LEADERSHIP TIPS

LEADERSHIP TIPS

Why Can't They Just Do Their Jobs

GARY YOUNG

Library of Congress Control Number:		2008907325
ISBN:	Hardcover	978-1-4363-6342-6
	Softcover	978-1-4363-6341-9

This book was printed in the United States of America.

To order additional copies of this book, contact:
Xlibris Corporation
1-888-795-4274
www.Xlibris.com
Orders@Xlibris.com
51695

CONTENTS

ACKNOWLEDGMENTS

I would like to thank all the people whom I have worked with for the past fifty-five years, but most of them have expired. In one way or another, they've all contributed immeasurably to my understanding of family, life, and work and how interdependent and inseparable they are from one another. The names of those that have unknowingly contributed to this book would take several pages to compile, but they did so in ways they would never have imagined and, therefore, have my undying appreciation and respect regardless of their role in my learning.

I want to especially thank my wife, Anita, with whose help and encouragement I've have had the energy and inclination to accept this challenge. She has supported me and my idiosyncrasies for forty-eight years, following me from job to job, perhaps not always willingly but with quiet understanding, always making sure that we maintain our roots. I also want to thank all the other members of my family as well as my friends for years of patience and putting up with me and my obnoxiousness, never trying to change me, but accepting me as I am. In addition, I'd like to give a special thanks to David Harris and Fred Schreiber for suggesting that I may have information that would be a valuable tool for managers, supervisors, and employees that would help them understand the role of a leader and the issues leaders address on a daily basis.

They've all inspired me to put in print the things that I've observed and learned about people and their perceptions, experiences, and opinions of the world of work.

INTRODUCTION

"In the beginning was the word, and the word was leadership." I believe that may have been a scripture quotation, or maybe it was something I heard Joe Hamixx from the Bronx say during one of his philosophical rants. Nevertheless, the central question to this journey to discover the true meaning of leadership is what's a leader and what exactly is leadership.

To begin to understand, we must first understand some of the perceptions of what a leader is and when to place the label of leadership on the activities of those entrusted with the responsibility to lead. Much has been researched and written regarding leadership. For example, when someone declares themselves the leader, are they drawing that conclusion from their skills and abilities or from their position? If it's from a position of power, they may have no leadership ability at all. We find this to be true in many organizations, both in the public and private sectors. Therefore, I've included much of the research in this manuscript. Many researchers are unwitting contributors to this exercise, but their views and insight are invaluable. Couple their research with personal longtime observations made in over fifty-five years in the workforce in a plethora of different jobs from cleansing soles in a shoe factory, selling Kirby vacuum cleaners, meat cutting, grocery stocking, archivist, library assistant, film editor, meteorologist, service station attendant, personnel specialist, manpower analyst, and management advisor, their claims have been validated. I think you'll find the leadership qualities and values described here unarguably sound.

A DEFINITION OF LEADERSHIP

In his book *Working with Emotional Intelligence*, Daniel Goleman defines "leadership" as the ability to inspire and guide individuals and groups. He describes leaders as having the following competencies:

- Leaders are articulate and arouse emotion for a shared vision and mission.
- Leaders step forward to lead as needed.
- Leaders guide the performance of others while holding them accountable.
- Leaders lead by example.

Where do you rate on each of these?

WHAT IS THE PERFECT LEADER, AND DOES HE OR SHE EXIST?

To paraphrase W. Somerset Maugham, "There are three rules for creating good leaders. Unfortunately, no one knows what they are."

There's no perfect leader. That's why good leaders are always trying to improve themselves through self-study, training, education, mentorship, making mistakes, and then learning from them, etc. Since there are no perfect leaders, it's hard to build a good leadership model. That's why there are hundreds of them. But we can be sure of a few things the good leaders posses:

- A vision of the future (where they're going).
- The ability to encourage followers to jump into that experience (work through the many changes required to achieve that vision).

11

- A love of self-improvement for themselves and their followers. This desire makes them good coaches and mentors.
- Empowering their followers to get things done (delegation).
- If you're a leader who can be trusted, then those around you will grow to respect you. To be such a leader, there is a leadership framework to guide you:

BE a professional. Examples: Be loyal to the organization, perform selfless service, and take personal responsibility.

BE a professional who possess good character traits. Examples: Honesty, competence, candor, commitment, integrity, courage, straightforwardness, imagination.

KNOW the four factors of leadership: follower, leader, communication, and situation.

KNOW yourself. Examples: strengths and weakness of your character, knowledge, and skills.

KNOW human nature. Examples: human needs, emotions, and how people respond to stress.

KNOW your job. Examples: be proficient and be able to train others in their tasks.

KNOW your organization. Examples: where to go for help, its climate and culture, who the unofficial leaders are.

DO:

DO provide direction. Examples: goal setting, problem solving, decision making, planning.

DO implement. Examples: communicating, coordinating, supervising, evaluating.

DO motivate. Examples: develop morale and sprit in the organization, train, coach, counsel.

LEADERSHIP QUALITIES

Bookstores are full of books, magazines, CDs, and audiotapes describing and prescribing leadership. A general theme can quickly be recognized: *anyone can be a leader*. Leaders aren't born. The traits aren't genetically instilled – leaders make themselves by developing key traits and skills. What are some of the traits of a good leader that you can work to develop in yourself?

Among many:

- Leaders motivate other people to perform at their highest level (maximum potential).
- Leaders are consistent in actions, moods, and words.
- Leaders are trustworthy.

CHARACTERISTICS OF A GREAT LEADER

As I said earlier, great leaders are not born. They create themselves by working to develop certain qualities and skills. In *Leadership for Dummies*, Marshall Loeb and Stephen Kindell list several characteristics important to leadership:

- **Leaders are eager.** They approach tasks readily and gladly. They're excited by the challenge. They step forward even when the task is onerous, daunting, or does nothing to enhance their careers.
- **Leaders are cheerful.** They're able to stay positive despite adversity (even if they don't get the satisfaction they were looking for).
- **Leaders are honest.** They're authentic and communicate openly and directly. There's never any mistake about what was said or intended.

In *Real Leaders Drink Their Coffee Black*, Dr. Michael Lindquist describes some distinguishing principles of leadership this way:

> **Take care of what others don't.** Treat diligently the things in life that other people don't notice, and you'll automatically take care of those areas that everyone notices. Acknowledgment does matter. So does the promptly returned phone call or e-mail that tells people that you're busy – but not too busy for them. It's a simple act that shows deep respect for their time and will ensure their undivided attention.
>
> **Real leaders never shout.** Whenever a leader angrily loses control, it reinforces everyone's opinion that they were never in control to

begin with. You never have to put someone in his or her place to prove you're in charge.

Time matters. Some things can often be recovered, but never a lost opportunity. What can be said in thirty minutes or less should be said. Starting meetings on time communicates that you value people's schedules. Some leaders come to meetings late because they squeeze too much activity into too little time frames. If you come in unprepared and unsettled you express to those that were on time that you have little respect for them.

Correct problems that aren't yours. What many step over as a nuisance, a leader takes responsibility for. The simplest way to achieve prosperity is to find a way to solve someone else's problem.

No one wants to break a $100 bill. It's always more cost efficient to retain an existing customer than to find a new one. The same is true with friendships. The investment it takes to keep a loyal relationship solid is much easier than it is too emotionally start. What we hold on to the longest, increases in value. Hold on to your integrity; then you can pass it on to your successors.

Admitting a mistake takes more than words; it takes guts. You know you can trust a person who is secure enough to take blame and humble enough to see the value of repairing damaged relationships with two simple words: I'm sorry. Apologies are good measures of our pride index. The harder it is to admit a mistake, the higher the probability we'll continue to make it over and over again. People are more willing to forgive and move on when there is an honest apology. Truthful people know they could have made similar mistakes or under the right circumstances done much worse.

Leaders buy things before they need them. Waiting until you've got to replace something almost always results in paying too much. When you see a sale and you know it's a useful item you'll eventually need, buy it – cheaper. Likewise, leaders plan for retirement when they're in their prime.

Leaders deal in oil – 10W-40, not crude. Taking the time to regularly change the oil in your car is a nuisance, but it's always smarter and cheaper than changing engines; as a Fram oil filter commercial once claimed, "You can pay me now, or pay me later."

Hiring someone carefully today saves the potential frustration of later having to fire them. Occasionally, changing policy, vision, goals, and customer service rules can result in long-range benefits that are much more valuable.

Leaders notice the condition of restrooms. It's the room everyone uses and no one wants to clean. You can tell what a leader thinks – not by the vision statement on the wall – but by the detail put into nonessentials like bathroom cleanliness. It's the places in our lives that we don't want to talk about that make the difference between getting by and getting to the top. Closing the door may temporarily keep the smell from wafting out, but eventually, someone is going to have to open that door and take a look at the parts of our lives that are all too human. If we're honest about the unpleasant sides of our personalities and diligent in the areas we'd rather forget about, we may find that a whole lot of people will appreciate us and trust us more.

Leaders control what's allowed into their minds. You can't change someone's opinion of you, and you don't want to give others the power to influence your opinion of them either. Seven percent of our communication is done verbally. The other 93 percent is accomplished through body language and tone of voice. We're easily influenced by other's words; use the wisdom to know which ones you'll allow to remain in your memory.

Leaders don't join organizations just to cooperate. If you're a true leader, you're not content to meekly follow the "pipers." You join in order to help build, morph, or lead into greatness. What makes most unifying meetings successful is when everyone puts aside the uniqueness that made them great. F-15s fly alone. They don't fit in well with crop dusters. If you feel out of place in meetings, it's because you are. You shine, however, in those meetings where you dare to dream out loud. Don't cooperate as much as compete. *Competition* isn't a dirty word. Done with integrity, it produces higher quality products and honest, long-term relationships.

PERSONALITY TYPES

The Golden Rule of "treating others as you like to be treated" isn't always the best way to deal with your employees. In fact, it may be effective only with people who are very similar to you. For instance, the things that might influence you may antagonize someone else. Leaders know they are much more successful if they tailor their communication to accommodate others' personality styles. When you approach someone, quickly try to surmise whether that person is more introverted or extroverted, more sensing or intuitive, more thinking or feeling, more judging or perceptive. It'll make communication easier for you to understand the type of person you're dealing with. Each person is a combination of these four styles, therefore, may be difficult to read at any given time. Knowing your type helps in recognizing the styles of others and how they may be different under different conditions. (I'm still trying to figure out what type I am generally. My wife has some suggestions that aren't on this list however.)

LEADERS MAKE EYE CONTACT

Leaders know there is more to communication than just talking. Body language is just as important as the verbal message. Body language is comprised of such things as posture and facial expressions, including eye contact. Looking someone directly in the eye is a sign of self-respect and mutual respect. When making eye contact, you're acknowledging the importance of the other person. Eye contact shows that you are confident and willing to give someone your full attention.

LEADERSHIP IS ENERGY

Leaders set the emotional tone and pace for their organizations. Successful leaders give off a high level of positive energy that envelops the organization. The more positive and energetic the leader, the more positive, cooperative, and productive the team members will be. To see this in action, think about the pace and energy level of your team the next time you're feeling physically or emotionally drained.

CONDUCT A PERSONAL INVENTORY

Contrary to what you may believe, leadership positions are demanding. By their nature, they require the application of specific knowledge, skills, and qualities to any given situation. Before you accept such a position, be sure you're a match for its demands. Ask specifically what is expected of you, not only in terms of results, but also in personal qualities and traits you need to bring to the job.

One way to do this is by conducting a personal inventory of your strengths and weaknesses in relation to the position you're considering. List everything you know about what you're expected to bring to the job – what you are good at, and in which are you not so adept. Be brutally honest and list everything. When you're finished, evaluate the weaknesses for those you can change (and at what cost) and those you can't. Now you're ready to make a decision, confident in your abilities, and know where you need to improve.

KNOW WHY YOU'RE VALUED

You're competing for a promotion you've been preparing for your entire career. With this job, you join the executive-managerial ranks. If you're being considered for a leadership position, it's safe to assume that someone recognizes your specific skills. But what are those skills and don't you need to know what they are in order to successfully lead your team? During your interview and any subsequent meetings before accepting the position, if offered, ask open-ended questions that compel the interviewer to respond. For example, ask, "What skills do you think are most important to successfully complete this project?" With questions like this, you'll learn why you're being considered and what will be expected of you.

RISK TAKERS

There's a little Sherlock Holmes in every good leader.

"Leaders, especially top managers, are calculated risk-takers. They get ahead by knowing when to say yes, and they stay ahead by knowing when to say no." (Quinn Kroll, Pull Technologies Inc.)

A good leader knows that one of his/her most important skills is being able to quickly grasp a situation and evaluate the potential outcome. Evaluation means being able to see the strengths and weaknesses of the situation and the advantages and disadvantages for taking action. Key to being an expert evaluator is the ability to be a good listener and a thorough researcher.

SUCCESS IS NEVER ACCIDENTAL

Lou Holtz was a successful football coach for more than twenty-five years. As he achieved record after record, he writes in his book, *Winning Every Day: The Game Plan for Success,* that he learned one very important thing: winning is never accidental. To win consistently, you must have a clear plan and intense motivation. Holtz believes champions are not born – they are made. Here are some of the coach's tips to help be more successful:

- Know what you want. *Commit* yourself and your people to reaching specific goals.
- Be appropriately tough. If you want to achieve great things, you have to *set lofty goals*. Hold yourself and your employees *accountable* to do whatever's necessary to reach those goals.
- Have an open-door policy. Being a leader doesn't mean knowing all the answers. Show your willingness to *be available*, to *listen*, and to *be receptive to ideas*.

BE THE VISION

Successful leaders are passionate about what they do. Not only is it important for leaders to be engrossed in their jobs, but it's also vital that they are totally committed to the mission and vision of their organization or team. Leaders are expected to personify the vision of what must be achieved. They, *by their actions and words*, must be an example of what it takes to accomplish goals and objectives. You can't fake your commitment. *If you can't own the organization's vision, don't expect your employees to be dedicated to it or to believe in you.*

"Failure is not permanent and neither is success." (Michael Altshuler, Boynton Beach, FL.)

TURNING VISION INTO GOALS

Once an organization has defined its vision, the task of putting the dream into action begins. Vision is the responsibility of an organization's leadership, including planning for its accomplishment. Try the following steps to begin the planning process:

- Briefly describe the idea behind your organization. (Why does it exist?)
- Now summarize the vision that drives the idea. (What was intended when established?)
- Next, list all the reasons your organization will be successful. (What is good and how does that contribute to completion of the mission?)
- Finally, describe how you as a leader can contribute to making the vision a reality. Repeat this all the way down the organizational chart, involving everyone and enlisting each person's commitment to success (those not committed are your weak links and should be replaced – kinda like the flapper ball in your toilet when it begins to

leak – pull it out and replace it with a new one. That's not a threat of forced commitment, just reality of today's work world. There's neither time nor place on the job for baby sitting, regardless of how old the babies are.

EMOTIONAL INTELLIGENCE

Leaders work to their highest level. But in order to maintain their personal productivity, they constantly look for new trends in time management, learning, and other things. In his book *Working with Emotional Intelligence*, Daniel Goleman also shows how managing our emotions can help us reach our highest level of competence at work. Emotional intelligence is how we deal with the softer side of things in our work lives, i.e., dealing with people, managing relationships, and understanding ourselves. Using emotional intelligence, managers can develop a finer sense of how other people feel and what they need in order to appropriately motivate them.

WHAT IS EMOTIONAL INTELLIGENCE?

- The ability to perceive accurately, appraise, and express emotion
- The ability to access or generate feelings when they facilitate thought
- The ability to understand emotion and emotional knowledge
- The ability to regulate emotions to promote emotional and intellectual growth

ELEMENTS OF EMOTIONAL INTELLIGENCE

Personal Competencies:

- Self-Awareness: knowing one's internal likes/dislikes, preferences, resources, and intuitions
- Managing Emotions: managing one's internal states, impulses, and resources
- Motivation: emotional tendencies that guide or facilitate reaching goals

Social Competencies:

- Empathy: awareness of others' feelings, needs, and concerns
- Social Skills: adeptness at inducing desirable responses in others.

WHAT IS YOUR EMOTIONAL INTELLIGENCE?

Goleman tells managers that to be effective with others and to be most productive themselves, they must know how to use emotions and feelings appropriately. He says that emotional intelligence is twice as important for top performance as IQ and technical expertise combined. In fact, he says, the higher up the corporate ladder, the more critical emotional intelligence becomes, accounting for nearly 90 percent of success in leadership positions. Emotional intelligence depends on how well you master five competencies:

- **Self-awareness** or knowing how you feel and accurately assessing your abilities
- **Self-regulation** or the ability to handle and manage your emotions
- **Motivation** or knowing what drives you to excel
- **Empathy** or your awareness of the feelings of others
- **Social skills** or how you handle relationships

EMOTIONALLY INTELLIGENT ORGANIZATIONS

The emotionally intelligent work group or organization has a culture that exhibits

- organizational self-awareness of its internal and external needs;
- management of organizational emotions through leadership and environment;
- organizational motivation through meaningful work and the delivery of incentives;
- organizational empathy by maintaining effective and meaningful relationships with customers and employees; and
- mentoring of organizational social skills through training, productive personnel selection practices, and performance appraisals.

Every large organization has a number of employees who are capable of identifying better ways of doing things. Just about everyone else has good ideas from time to time as well. Employees would like to feel that their ideas can make a difference in their workplace. For many people, in fact, there are few things more motivating than seeing – and assisting with – the successful implementation of an idea they suggested.

Managers who are aggressive about eliciting the ideas of their staff find that getting everyone involved in the effort to improve the operation has an incredible multiplier effect on the rapidity of the change process and the commitment of employees to those changes. To do this, managers need to foster a climate of openness that gets employees engaged in the process of innovation and organizational renewal.

These are a few practices that, implemented together, represent an integrated approach to innovation and motivation that has proven to be very effective.

1. **Get to Know Every Employee**

    It's virtually impossible for a manager to motivate his/her employees without getting to know them. Whenever starting a new job, all managers should make a point of having a one-on-one meeting with each member of their staff. Managers who don't know what makes each employee tick will find it difficult to motivate them. Similarly, if the manager doesn't know an employee's strengths, he'll be unlikely to find the right role for them. These one-on-one sessions are an opportunity to encourage employees to contribute their ideas.

2. **Challenge Them to Improve the Operation**

    One way for managers to make it clear that they welcome input and suggestions is to give each employee clear instructions in their work requirements to take a hard look at the whole operation and make recommendations for improvements. This establishes a provision that all employees are expected to contribute their ideas. It's equally important to comment on each employee's efforts in this area at evaluation time.

3. **"Customer for a Day"**

    Another mechanism a manager can use to elicit suggestions is to have each employee be "customer for a day." In work centers that have customers, whether internal or external, it can be enlightening to look at the operation from the client's point of view. The most engaged and creative employees will probably identify a long list of things that can be improved to make the customer's experience more comfortable, transparent, and efficient. At a minimum, the experience will sensitize employees of any hardships experienced by the customer. (Note: Employees wouldn't really be "customer" for the whole day. But they should be given sufficient time to go all the way through the process and then to write up their impressions and suggestions for the supervisor.)

4. **Don't Forget the Implementation**

    A crucial part of this whole equation is the actual implementation of the great ideas generated by employees. Without follow-through, the organization simply ends up with a long list of unused suggestions and a lot of frustrated employees. To the extent possible, managers should put the person who suggested an idea in charge of the actual implementation. The initiator of an innovative idea usually has a sense of ownership and is highly motivated to see their suggestion put into effect. Those managers who try to take the lead on all new initiatives will find themselves overworked and unable to accomplish everything they would like to accomplish. By delegating the implementation, the managers can give their employees a terrific developmental opportunity, with the manager just needing to provide guidance and support.

These are just a sample of methods for encouraging employees to contribute their ideas for improving their organization. Implemented on their own, each of these practices would have limited impact. The key is to use a multifaceted approach that continually reinforces the fact that employees' ideas are welcome, valued, and rewarded.

WHAT'S YOUR AQ?

That's right – what's your AQ, not IQ. Dr. Paul Stoltz, in his book *Adversity Quotient: Turning Obstacles into Opportunities* has developed a measure of how people cope with adversity called the adversity quotient or AQ. Here are two dimensions that make up the core of a high AQ, or the ability to turn adversity into opportunity.

- **Control**. How much control do you feel you have over adverse situations? To what extent do you feel you can influence the outcomes? People with high AQs *always* feel that they are in – at least some – control and even in overwhelming situations will devise a plan and attack the elements over which they feel they have some control.
- **Ownership**. To what extent do you feel you're responsible for the problem and accountable for a solution? People with high AQs are willing to step up and deal with the problem, regardless of who or what caused it.

DON'T OVERFOCUS

Successful people tend to be involved in many different things, for the most part doing a good job with all of them. The trick is to know when you've got just enough on your plate or when you're overextended. Leaders focus their efforts, make goals, and set out to reach them. The thrill of achievement can be exhilarating and addictive, creating a life that may soon get out of balance.

If you're an overachiever, look carefully at all the things you're attempting to do and ask yourself one simple question: Does the cost outweigh the benefit or vice versa? If the price is too high, dump the activity and move on to a less stressful life.

MOTIVATING SKEPTICAL EMPLOYEES

Leaders must often sell their vision for the organization to disgruntled employees whose skepticism can come from a myriad of sources. For example, maybe leaders in the past were unqualified or not trustworthy. Whatever the reasons, leaders must get employees to commit to the mission and goals of the project at hand. Leaders sell their agendas to employees in many ways, including the following:

- By *breaking down projects into tasks* that employees can see and are capable of being accomplished.
- By *being honest* and up-front with regards to the challenges but optimistic that the team can succeed.
- By *having a plan* for reaching your goals. Show employees you know where you're going and how to get there.

DIFFERENCES BETWEEN MANAGERS AND LEADERS

In his book, *What Leaders Really Do*, Harvard business professor John Kotter describes the differences between managers and leaders. According to Kotter, *managers cope with complexity* and *leaders cope with change. Management is concerned with controlling people while leadership focuses on motivating people.* He believes that organizations tend to be *overmanaged and underled*, and he suggests that more be done to promote cultures of leadership within organizations. He recommends early career challenges and a broad-based range of experiences as being instrumental in developing effective leaders. If management is aware of the different skills required, it is possible to train employees to fill both roles.

BE AN EFFECTIVE COACH

Leading a team to success takes more than setting goals and knowing how to make them happen. Successful leaders are also good coaches. That is, leaders recognize that success is as dependent on their employees as it is on their personal skills and knowledge. To be a good coach, you must be committed to everyone's growth and success, not just your own. You must do everything you can to remove barriers that prohibit employee growth. Coaches don't dictate – *they encourage and support.*

LEADERS WEAR MANY HATS

To be successful, leaders must be multitalented. To turn a vision into reality, a leader must be willing and able to assume a wide variety of roles, easily stepping in and out of each as a project evolves. Consider your ability to perform in the following roles:

- **Truth seeker.** If maneuvering through unknown areas, do you have the *huevos* to know and adhere to important values and principles? Can you instill this strength of character in others?
- **Direction setter.** Can you determine a path to reach the goals that have been set? Can you educate and motivate others to follow your lead?
- **Change agent.** If big changes are made, can you show strength and optimism? Can you help others see the need for changes and enlist their support and commitment?

MORE ROLES OF LEADERS

Previously, I described various roles that leaders may have to assume in order to change a vision into a reality. Sometimes leaders must be truth seekers, direction setters, and change agents. Now consider your ability to perform these additional roles:

- **Spokesperson.** Leaders must represent their organizations, teams, visions, and goals to everyone else. They are the ones that communicate values to others.
- **Coach.** Leaders must champion each individual person on their teams, doing whatever they must do to ensure employee success.
- **Team builder.** Leaders must have the knowledge and skills to meld a disparate group of individuals into an effective team.

INGREDIENTS FOR EXCELLENCE

Leaders exhibit excellence in everything they do. Robert Worden describes various ingredients for excellence at his company Eastman Kodak as qualities that hold true for leaders everywhere as follows:

- Present your case convincingly and passionately.
- Have high energy and be willing to make personal sacrifices.
- Sense personal and organizational sensitivities.
- Be able to take creative risks and adapt.
- Inspire and guide other people.
- Be proactive and action oriented.

CHARISMA

Many leaders exhibit a high degree of charisma. However, there is a difference between charisma and manipulation. To be truly charismatic, a leader must be authentic. Charisma involves several factors – being sincere about one's beliefs, being able to feel passionate about them, and being able to communicate that passion. Believing in your message and its value to the group's welfare is what separates a charismatic leader from a self-serving, manipulative one.

MOTIVATION

The best leaders have an almost magical ability to turn a phrase and articulate their agenda for the organization graphically, compellingly, memorably.

– Robert Kaplan, Center for Creative Leadership

In other words, it takes more than simple power to motivate and lead a group. As Kaplan indicates, leaders *excite* people's imaginations and *inspire* them to move in a desired direction. People feel respected and free to manage their tasks – they are *empowered* to contribute.

POWER AND INFLUENCE

Whether or not you occupy a leadership role, there are times you must motivate others to do what you want. There are two ways to get others to act by using *power* or *influence*. Knowing the difference can make you much more effective in motivating others:

- When people give you your way out of fear or respect, it's because you've used your power – either forcibly or informally – to persuade them.
- When you use influence, you motivate others to do what you want by steering them toward wanting the same goals that you do.

What's the better way to effect lasting change? *Use influence to get others' commitments to your goals.*

NICE GUYS DON'T FINISH LAST

When it comes to leadership, the old saying "nice guys finish last" isn't true. In an extensive study comparing superior to average leadership, the U.S. Navy reported that the very best commands were those led by – you guessed it – *nice guys*. The best leaders were able to balance a *people-oriented* personable style with *decisive* management. The most *effective leaders* were also more *positive* and *outgoing*; more *expressive* and *dramatic*; *warmer* and more *sociable*; *friendlier* and more *democratic*; more *cooperative*, *likeable*, *appreciative*, and *trustworthy*.

KNOWING WHEN TO BE TOUGH

Effective leaders know *when to be assertive and when to be kindly* and less direct when guiding and influencing. Sometimes leadership demands being *tough*. Being the nice guy doesn't get the job done. When being tough, there are two potential failures for leaders. Does your leadership suffer from either one?

- Failure to *be emphatically assertive* when you need to be. The danger here is falling into the trap of passively *accepting poor performance* because you as a leader *want to be everyone's friend*. (Do we know supervisors like that?) Be friendly but keep a professional distance.

- The inability to *be clear and firm.* If you don't set the pace and communicate goals and responsibilities clearly, workers won't know what's expected of them and *morale* – as well as *productivity* – will be seriously affected.

DARE TO BE DIFFERENT – BE CREATIVE

Creativity, according to Roger von Oech, author of *A Whack on the Side of the Head,* is all about breaking free from the everyday norms of society and daring to be different, not being afraid to free the mind and cultivate the imagination. He says that taking a figurative "whack on the side of the head" means stepping back and looking at things in a different way.

Creative workers challenge the establishment (regular routine), take risks, and explore new areas, while at the same time remaining receptive to new ideas and change. They know that true innovations come from creative inspiration, not from stubborn adherence to routines. Creative managers encourage their employees to try new ways of doing things – just because something is done one particular way doesn't mean there isn't another way to do it (but try convincing the human resources office of that). The ability to connect two or more unrelated ideas to form a new one is the sign of true creative brilliance.

EMOTIONAL INTELLIGENCE REVISITED

For years, training has focused on the technical skills to enhance or nurture an employee's leadership and managerial capabilities. Now attention is being focused on softer areas such as interpersonal skills and psychological traits. Research shows that the farther one rises on the corporate ladder, the more important emotional intelligence skills are to success.

Key emotional intelligence variables include those of self-awareness, self-regulation, motivation, empathy, and social skills. Where do you rate yourself on each of these soft skills?

HANDLING CONFLICT

More than ever, today's workplace operates by team management. When you're working closely with others, conflict is certain to arise. When it does, try this to turn conflict into solutions:

- Openly discuss the problem and agree on an accurate description of the disagreement.

- Determine whether the problem is information or emotion based.
- Deal only with areas of disagreement; ask each person to elaborate on their thoughts and feelings.
- Identify areas of agreement.
- Find ways to compromise on areas of continuing disagreement.
- Restate the conflict in a positive solution statement and get everyone's approval.

Doesn't that sound like mediation? It isn't arbitration because an arbitrator would define the problem and tell you what the solution is, and then all parties would live with it, like it or not. The result would be that someone would be unhappy. In mediation, the parties settle their dispute and come to an agreement everyone can live with.

GENDER DIFFERENCES IN LEADERSHIP

Think of all the male and female bosses you've had in the past. Did they manage differently based on their gender? The gender-based differences in leadership styles is a topic Judy Rosener, author of *America's Competitive Secret: Women Managers*, has spent a lot of time researching.

She finds that men traditionally use "transactional leadership." In other words, men tend to act as distributors of rewards and punishment. Women, on the other hand, are more likely to use a transformational style. They tend to share power and information with their subordinates, and they encourage participative decision-making. She suggests that when organizations remain open to different interpretations of effective leadership, they can capitalize on the strengths and diversity of the entire organization.

For many reasons, leaders change. One indication of real leadership skills comes after a leader is gone (that's when those that are left get to blame you for everything that ever went wrong, back to 1937 or your sixteenth birthday, whichever came first). Thus, the final determination of a leader's abilities may rest on whether or not the processes and structures have been designed and used that mean the work can and will continue after his/her departure. To ensure that you pass on your knowledge to those that come after, consider these two techniques:

- **Write down** everything that's needed to ensure the person coming after you can pick up where you left off.
- **Train your successor**. You may not be able to select him/her, but you can teach them what you've accomplished and how. Be sure to share both the positives and negatives, the good and the bad.

According to Peter Drucker, 'Leadership is not a magnetic personality – that can just as well be a glib tongue. It is not 'making friends and influencing people' – that is flattery. Leadership is lifting a person's vision to higher sights, raising a person's performance to a higher standard, building personality beyond its normal limitations." Drucker contrasts leadership, "doing the right things," with management, "doing things right."

CUSTOMERS

The definition of *customer* is broader than ever. Customers are now considered to be anyone with whom you interrelate and communicate. Treating everyone as a customer puts things in a different perspective. Communications will be more thoughtful since you'll be always looking for ways to improve and maintain your relationships. To be more successful, identify all your customers – both internal and external.

- External customers are easy. They're the ones that buy your services or products, your suppliers, funding sources, etc.
- The idea of internal customers is a newer concept. They're the people you work with, i.e., your boss and other employees/coworkers.

A BETTER MEETING

Dorothy Leeds, president, Organizational Technologies, has an idea for making meetings more interesting and interactive. She suggests that meeting agendas be built around questions. Before the meeting, circulate a memo with topics to be discussed. Ask participants to prepare questions that need to be addressed about these issues and start the meeting with them. During the meeting, Leeds says leaders need to ask more and talk less. End the meeting with summary questions that spur everyone to action and further consideration/discussion.

SIMPLIFY TO BEAT STRESS

Stress at work often comes from placing too many demands on ourselves and having unrealistic expectations. If, as a result, your life is too complicated and you're feeling burned out, then it's time for you to simplify. Here are some suggestions to help you master your emotions, energy, and time at work and at home:

- Block off at least fifteen minutes a day to plan your priorities for that day and make a commitment to accomplish them. Stay focused.
- Focus on the present. Forget the past and disregard the future. As long as you're doing your best now, there's no reason to worry about tomorrow.
- Make a to-do list. Now force yourself to cross one thing off your list without doing it! This lets you see your work assignments from a new perspective – you may have been treating things as emergencies that really weren't.

KNOW YOUR POPULARITY GOAL

Some people are perfectly happy just doing their job (and nothing more) and blending into the society with everyone else. Others want to be popular, even famous (as opposed to infamous) for what they do. Knowing your need for popularity can help smooth the way to job success. If you want above-average levels of recognition, here are some ways to get it:

- Find what you're good at and stick with it.
- Develop a good reputation by creating an image of what you'd like to be known for.
- Look for tasks and projects that make you look good and work hard to be the best.

Be consistent. Bring something good to your work team, and you'll soon be recognized for your dependability and contribution.

MAINTAINING A GOOD REPUTATION

Maintaining a good reputation is important to career success (this should be obvious). From the secretary to the CEO, reputations can affect growth as people and employees. Some tips on keeping a good reputation from Mike Paul, a professor at New York University:

- Learn humility. If you've screwed up, admit it. Don't brag about your successes. Let someone else do it for you.
- Be accountable. Take responsibility for your mistakes. Put yourself in someone else's shoes when reviewing your behavior.
- Understand what the truth really means. Never make a statement with a "but" in it. That means you're not really holding yourself accountable. Admit mistakes, learn from them, and move on.

- Expand your horizons. One way to improve reputation is by helping others. Volunteer for difficult work assignments. Get involved helping others complete theirs. The idea here is to be known as someone who cares.

MESSING WITH YOUR JOB

In today's economy, it may be better to try to find ways to make your current job work for you than to look for a new one. Here are some tips on ways to improve your current situation:

- **Focus on how you're doing, not on what you're doing.** Too often we tend to relate to all the things we've got going, not how well we're doing on any one of them. If we do well on the "how" every time, the "what" will take care of itself.
- **Find a mentor.** Everyone can use someone with more experience to guide them. It isn't a sign of weakness to ask questions, it's a sign of intelligence to realize you don't know all the answers.
- **Combine you talents with the organization's goals.** Be sure you know what those goals are. This is one of our biggest problems, not easily overcome. Our goals may not be in sync with those of the organization. If they're not, how can you get together and establish what they are, stay within the limits of the law, and be productive?
- **Admit to at least one weakness** and try to overcome it. I have too many to focus on just one so I don't try to correct any of them. Is that a function of old age?
- **Create you own project.** I know there is little time for that, but there are some unanswered questions that could be researched; for example, I was asked a short time ago how does average grade (and grade creep) impact work-year funding from one fiscal year to the next? Good question. Many federal agencies discontinued tracking average grade years ago because grades, in and of themselves, didn't show how much it cost to do business. There are too many variables, i.e., between steps within grades, differences in position classification policy (?) or philosophy, numbers of overhires, etc., that were not identified. Therefore, grades didn't represent costs.

MAKE YOURSELF INDISPENSABLE

In a time of instability, how do you make yourself indispensable? Try these suggestions for maximizing your value at work:

- Spend half an hour each day researching trends in your work specialty.
- Ask management for ideas regarding what you can do to make yourself more valuable.
- Take work assignments no one else wants.

GETTING THINGS DONE

Some people are great at jumping in and getting things started. Finishing is a different story. Whether it's because of unrealistic expectations they place on themselves or their difficulty in staying attentive to long-term projects, completing tasks can be challenging. If this is familiar, here are some suggestions to try:

- Set deadlines for yourself. Focus your energies on achieving the deadline. Don't let your attention drift or let yourself procrastinate.
- If delegating tasks, tell people you need the work a day or two before you absolutely have to have it – they could have the same challenges in completing things.
- Be specific about the due date for projects. Instead of accepting "sometime this week" from your boss, decide a precise turn-in date and time.

CAN YOUR ORGANIZATION FUNCTION WITHOUT YOU?

How many of you think that your organization can't function without you? That's a common assumption, particularly among the annoyed and stressed out among us. The truth is that your work unit should be able to get along without you just fine. The next time you go on vacation or temporary duty somewhere, ask yourself this question when you return: how well did things go while I was gone? If the organization has suffered, maybe you should think more about how much you can delegate or how well you're sharing information. Also think about how you prepare others when you'll be out for a few days. Keeping information to yourself doesn't increase your value to the organization.

As researchers Warren Bennis and Burt Nanus noted in *Leaders*, "The problem with many organizations, and especially the ones that are failing, is that they tend to be over-managed and under-led."

This is especially true when so many bosses fail to create an environment that encourages managers to spend their time expanding and deepening their vision for the future of the organization. Great leaders understand that by positioning the managers they lead for success, they help guarantee the success of the organization.

There are two things that can be of immediate value in preparing for a change in organizational leadership, but only if acted upon:

First, we know that studies have shown that in organizations that have a track record for growing leaders of character and capability, it is the senior leaders themselves (not the training shops or human resources offices) who assume the responsibility for preparing the next generation.

Second, we know that leaders are grown not by the lessons learned in the classroom but by the lessons of experience – lessons gathered from challenging and varied job experiences and from significant relationships built with senior leaders (both good and bad). It is through these impact experiences and significant relationships that practical leadership capability is learned and where character is observed and shaped in the melting pot of reality.

These senior leaders that grow and nourish other leaders play a role of exemplar, of coach, of mentor, and even of teacher. They give their time and wisdom to help make meaning and learning out of experience and observation.

We also know that senior leaders have learned, to the benefit of all, that at least one common thread ties together these two absolutely fundamental principles: the lessons of experience and significant relationships.

A MEANINGFUL MISSION STATEMENT

Since 9/11, the way we look at and consider our roles in life and work have changed. People are now more focused on questions of meaning and value, both personally and professionally. Employees want to feel as if their jobs have value and that they are contributing to society in some purposeful way.

In challenging times, vision, mission, and values keep an organization strong. Engaging employees in the mission has never been more important, and communication among all levels of the organizational structure is the key. Employees can help by being expressive and responsive to management's requests for information regarding employee concerns, by suggesting ways to improve their (the organization's) environment and goals.

KNOW WHAT FIRES YOU UP

Working without knowing what truly motivates you is like sailing a boat without a rudder – your course is going to wander, and you may not reach your destination. Find a time to sit quietly with yourself or with a good coach. Set a time limit, maybe fifteen to twenty minutes. During this time, list everything that motivates you. Don't analyze; just brainstorm. Once you've made the list, rank the motivators from most influential to least influential. Now that you've prioritized, think about the list and the rankings. Do you feel comfortable with them? Do they accurately reflect what is most motivating for you? If so, find ways to build these motivators into your life and watch your performance improve.

THE CANDIDATE VERSUS THE INSIDER

Which would you say is better: hiring a job candidate/applicant who scored exceptionally well on an interview, or the internal candidate who has an above average, but not exceptional past performance record? According to a study by a Cornell University (Industrial and Labor Relations School) researcher and his colleagues, the best choice is the insider. The Cornell researchers say that past *performance appraisals* are by far more valid in predicting future job performance. Thus, in cases where there is *reliable, valid* information about an above-average candidate, that candidate should be selected over top external candidates who may have had stellar interviews. Moral of the story – *keep performance appraisals in mind as you conduct yourself in your job.* Keep in mind how your day-to-day performance will position you when evaluation time approaches.

MOVIN' ON UP

Have dreams to move on up to that spacious office in the executive suite, the one with "BOSS" on the door? Here are some ways to impress management as you pursue your goal:

- Devise ways to improve problem areas. Create a plan and share it with management.
- Offer to help coworkers with their projects after regular hours.
- Give others credit when things go well.

LESSONS FOR THOSE WANTING TO MOVE UP

These are from a commencement address Maria Shriver made to the College of the Holy Cross in Massachusetts:

- Pinpoint your passion and go with your feelings.
- People you work for – and with – are as important as what you do. Always be on the watch for mentors.
- Laughter makes life manageable. Be willing to laugh at situations and at yourself.

MORE SIGNS THAT YOU'RE PROMOTABLE

Do you know how to evaluate whether or not you're promotable? Knowing some of the variables that produce promotions can help you maneuver your way to the next level. Ask yourself the following questions:

- Does your boss respect and trust you? Is your work closely monitored by your boss, or are you allowed to work independently? (Levels of trust)
- Is there someone who can take over your job? Sometimes promotions are withheld because there isn't anyone else available to do your job.
- How powerful is your boss? A boss with considerable clout can impress top management on your behalf.

EVALUATION AS A FOUR-PART PROCESS

Performance evaluation time can be a stressful time for everyone involved. However, Leigh Branham, author of *Keeping the People Who Keep You in Work*, advises that turning the evaluation into a four-part process to be conducted throughout the year will make the process more productive for both employer and employee. Here is the process:

- The first part of the process is sitting down at the beginning of the appraisal cycle for a planning session between the two of you. Talk about goals, objectives, and expectations.
- The second part of the cycle takes up much of the year, with employees doing their jobs and the boss giving them continual feedback.
- The third part of the process is writing the evaluation. This requires the boss to be a coach, finding ways to help employees do better work.
- The last part of the process is a review meeting between both employer and employee to discuss what the worker has done right and wrong, how they have developed, and what could be done better.

MENTORING IS A STRATEGY FOR SUCCESS

Many organizations are discovering the value of mentoring, pairing experienced employees to educate and provide emotional support to novices. For employees, it can mean a smoother journey to the "management suite." Here are some of the functions mentoring can serve:

- It helps new employees develop the political savvy necessary to exceed in today's world. Mentoring is a great way to become instantly privy to behind-the-scenes information.
- It acquaints new employees with the organization.
- Mentors provide career advice and guidance.

BE A TEACHER/MENTOR!

- As a mentor, you provide advice, and you challenge others to reach goals. Successful people can always point to someone – a teacher, coach, or boss – who helped them out. Often mentors don't have supervisory responsibility for the individual they mentor. That enables them to be more candid and honest in their role.
- Respect, console, and encourage those who have lost the good fight (i.e. experienced failure). Show concern and appreciation for the fact they tried.
- Try a blast from the past! Ask the senior members of your organization to share experience handling tough decisions. These experiences not only provide context for the present, but may also lend insight to handling future problems.
- Demonstrate that you value learning in all its forms: on the job, self-study, classroom, seminar, or just observation. The best way to show that you value learning is to be a continual learner yourself.

TAKING RISKS

Leaders will tell you that being willing to take a risk is one of the key elements to success. The good news is that, if you're afraid of taking risks, you can train yourself to be daring.

Build confidence by taking small risks first and tackling more challenging things as your courage and confidence grow. Consider the likely consequences of any risk you may take, and identify the worst thing that can happen to you. Then look at your reasoning for why that's the worst thing – faulty reasoning sometimes causes us to "catastrophize," when actually, chances are slim that a catastrophe will occur.

As a wise philosopher once said (again I think it was Joe Hamixx from the Bronx), it's easier to get forgiveness than to get permission.

GIVING PRAISE

Getting praised at work can make your day as well as cause you to be a little more productive. Here are some suggestions for the proper way to praise another employee or coworker:

- **Have a reason**. As a boss, the purpose of praise is to increase morale and reinforce positive behavior. As an employee, praise the boss when you want to acknowledge admirable performance (I realize that may be an extremely rare event, but praising each other should be part of daily activities).
- **Be specific**. Don't give blanket praise. Let someone know exactly what project or task you're complimenting. This is especially important when the employee has been working on a particularly tough job.
- **Mean it**. Be honest and sincere with your compliments. Phony praise causes you to lose credibility.

LET THEM KNOW THEY'RE OKAY!

Everyone needs a little praise. Being complimented at work is no exception. Here are two tips on the proper way to give kudos to coworkers or your boss:

- Don't get carried away. Praising too much or too often weakens the impact. For instance, don't praise the boss when it's awards time! Congratulate coworkers that received awards – assume that they're justified and be proud of the people that got them.
- Know where to give it. It's okay to compliment fellow employees in public or private. But when warranted, praise the boss in private in order to avoid making him/her uncomfortable. It also keeps you from looking like a suck-up.

GOALS

Your thinking skills can be considered directional skills because they set the direction of your organization or unit. They provide vision, purpose, and goal definition. These are your eyes to the future, allowing you to recognize the need for change, when to make it, how to implement it, and how to manage it. You find vision by reaching for any available reason to change, grow and improve – find something that is not broken and make it better. Just as you perform preventive maintenance on you car, you must perform preventive maintenance on your organization. Don't believe the old adage "If it ain't broke, don't fix it." The people who do, go broke! Treat every project as a change effort. Treat every job as a new learning experience.

Good organizations convey a strong vision of where they will be in the future. As a leader, you have to get your people to trust you and be sold on your vision. To sell them on your vision, you need to possess energy and display a positive attitude that is contagious. People want a strong vision of where they are going and a strong someone to lead them there. No one wants to be stuck in a dead-end organization going nowhere or headed in the wrong direction. They want to be involved with a winner! Your people will get you there. You can't do it alone!

When setting goals, keep these things in mind:

- They should be reasonable and attainable.
- They should improve the organization.
- Everyone should be involved in the goal-setting process.
- A program should be developed to reach each goal.

A STEP-BY-STEP SOLUTION

Most employers expect their employees to solve problems that come up in their jobs. The cause of problems is sometimes difficult to determine. Here are some suggestions for getting to the root of a troublesome situation:

- State the *problem* in specific terms.
- State *what should be occurring* in specific terms.
- State specific *differences* between what is occurring now and what should be occurring.
- *That's the problem definition.*
- *Brainstorm* all possible causes for the problem.
- *Design* and *apply* test solutions and then *evaluate* the results.

EVERYONE MAKES MISTAKES!

Everyone makes mistakes. In fact, highly successful creative people make more mistakes than the rest of us because they're always trying new things and searching for better ways to do them. The difference is they face their mistakes squarely, learn from them, and move on. So cut yourself some slack and accept that you're not perfect.

ARE YOU SABOTAGING YOUR CAREER?

Anyone can make a mistake, but research shows that even some very talented people habitually sabotage themselves in consistent ways. Several self-sabotaging personality types have been identified:

- The hero – the hero works seventy hours a week to impress the boss and outshine everyone but ends up burning out from stress.
- The meritocrat – the meritocrat sees everything in terms of black-and-white and thinks decisions should be made on merit alone – absolutely no politics allowed.
- The bulldozer – the bulldozer will push over anyone who stands in his or her path to power and glory.

Managers, supervisors, and employees alike should examine their behaviors at work for signs of self-sabotage. Even successful people do things that keep them from being fully successful.

ARE YOU AMONG THESE?

- The pessimist – the pessimist constantly resists change and is always negative. The pessimist negatively impacts everyone's morale.
- The rebel – the rebel constantly fights authority and resists being controlled.
- The home run hitter – the home run hitter is always focused on the long-term and grandiose results, frequently overlooking short-term attainable goals.

YOUR OWN WORST ENEMY

Here are some positive ways to sabotage your creativity:

- Don't look for a second right answer; go with your first thought.
- Drag your feet implementing, and don't make a commitment to doing what it takes to make your idea a success.
- Overanalyze an idea. Run it through one or more committees. Wait for full analysis.
- Hold lengthy meetings to explore the merits of any idea.

GET CREATIVE

One of the best ways to cope with organizational change (or any change as far as that goes) is to rev up your natural powers for creative intervention. Morton C. Orman, MD, says most problems are amenable to creative, innovative solutions. The thing that usually keeps these solutions from coming up is our own internal barriers and self-imposed restrictions. Dr. Orman says creative problem-solving always involves risks because proposing new ideas invites criticism. What if the idea fails? What if things end up worse than before? What if . . . ?

SO WHAT?!

You've got to be willing to accept risks if you're going to be free to think creatively. Trust yourself and others around you to recognize really bad ideas before they are implemented. Then give yourself the opportunity to think creatively – allowing any and all ideas to develop. Many organizations have regular brainstorming sessions for just this purpose. During times of reorganization and change, and change is inevitable, these creative sessions are especially important. Time should be set aside to make them a common occurrence.

KEEPING BUSY

When things are slow at work (and there are times that they are), the temptation is to be a little lazy. The best thing you can do at times like these is to keep yourself busy, looking for things to do to make the organization better. Some suggestions:

- Write ideas, quotes, numbers – anything you find inspirational – on a scrap of paper or enter into the computer for easy access in order to retrieve them later when you need a fresh thought.
- Confer with coworkers from other sections and talk with them for fresh perspectives on *work problems*.
- Take a vacation during the slow times so you're available at work when things pick up when you're really needed.

NO MORE PROCRASTINATION

If you always leave work projects until the last minute, you could be a habitual procrastinator. Unfortunately for you, procrastination is not a successful career strategy.

Beating procrastination requires both cultivating time-management skills and relearning some thought patterns, according to Michelle Tullier, PhD. She says, to beat procrastination, you must identify, challenge, and change the thoughts that continually lead you to delay things; and don't try to change on your own – network with other procrastinators.

LISTENING: A WINNING STRATEGY

To be a successful communicator is about much more than what you say. It's also about the ability to listen to others. Being a thoughtful listener can be a winning strategy. Here are some reasons you should pay more attention to listening:

- You'll be more competent. Listening is a way to gather information. The more information you have, the better you'll be able to do your job.
- You'll be in the loop. If you're always talking, you won't be fully aware of what's going on around you. Listening tells you what's happening – it keys you into what's going on with others, in your team, and organization at large.

"The more I listen to others, the more sense they begin to make." (Thad Russell)

LEADERSHIP PROBLEMS AND PITFALLS

Just because someone is in a leadership role doesn't mean they always lead effectively. Here are some common problems that may keep leaders from realizing their potential:

- They seek approval from others in the organization, particularly from those higher up. They make their decisions based on what others think or say.
- They are *argumentative* or *distrustful*. They may also be skeptical, tense, and possibly even paranoid. They are focused on their own interests and are likely to resist coaching or other feedback.

Have you heard of the Peter principle (I'm sure you all have) – that people are promoted to their level of inefficiency? Leaders have problems realizing their success also. Here are some common pitfalls:

- Leaders could be arrogant and too self-assured or confident, causing them to not listen or to dismiss feedback from others.
- They look for attention and excessively promote themselves. They brag about their successes and refuse to see their shortcomings and where they have failed. If they failed, it was someone else's fault.

OTHER PITFALLS

For the past two sections, I've discussed the common pitfalls that leaders encounter causing them to not realize their potential. Here are a few more that keep leaders from real success:

- They are impulsive, impatient, and unpredictable, and are inclined to act before considering the consequences of their actions. They make decisions based on speed, not on appropriateness or accuracy.
- They are perfectionistic, causing them to micromanage. They are controlling and demanding of others, and are often rigid in accepting new ideas or experimenting.

This contribution to *Leadership Tips* is a collaborative effort between Chuck Wilkson and me. He got to thinking of his own rules for conducting business and came up with some great ideas that I'm able to incorporate with mine. When they're followed, they work.

- **Be humble.** You may be good at what you do, but you're not that good. There is always someone out there a little brighter, a little quicker. There are only two kinds of people infallible: human resource managers, and I forgot who the others are. When dealing with people, you have to be likable to get things done.
- **Keep it simple.** Keep what simple? Everything. Reduce the job to parts and the parts to pieces. People have to follow, and buy into, your blinding logic. If it's too blinding, you lose supporters and followers.
- **Study the work of others.** You don't have to reinvent the wheel every time. Look at what worked elsewhere. It might work for you as well.
- **Don't be a 70 percenter.** You're getting paid. Work for it. A lot of folks go through the motions without putting much into their work. Things will slide, and you may get away with it for a while. People are tolerant, but they ain't dumb. They see what's going on. Why would anyone want to work for someone who doesn't care?
- **Keep a notebook.** Inspiration comes at the strangest times (at least it does for me – you can see where mine comes from). So do instructions and requests. Responding to the ad hoc stuff as well as the formal will get you a label of *reliable*.
- **Blow you own horn.** Just don't do it loudly. If you design a process that saves time or money, share it with your boss and peers. Don't let your project be like that described by Thomas Gray in his "Elegy Written in a Country Churchyard," "a flower is born to blush unseen, and waste its sweetness on the desert air" (waxing poetic).
- **Be a schmoozer.** Talk to people. Visit them where they work. The more that people hear, the more likely that they will listen and pay attention. They may even agree with you.
- **Write articles.** Get you ideas in print. Not everyone will be there when you talk. They may, however, read what you write. The avenues are there: the Web page, computerized letters, e-mail, etc.
- **Put family first.** Spouses and children are more important than careers. You may be working to support your family, but *they* also need time with you. Leave your work at the office and enjoy those you are working to support.

LEARN FROM YOUR FAILURES

When it comes to failure, society doesn't always understand. According to management professors Paul Nutt and Charles Manz, studying and writing about failure extensively, we live and work in a blame mentality. However, they say that to be a success, you have to be prepared to risk failure and equipped to constructively deal with it when it happens. Here are their suggestions:

- When faced with mistakes, accept them. You may feel like sweeping them under the carpet, denying them, or justifying them, but don't do it – accept responsibility.
- Look at the failure and ask what you can learn from it. Every mistake carries within it the opportunity to learn something new.
- If you must go to your boss, take a full description of the problem, what you've learned from it and suggestions for how to deal with things in the future.

SUCCESS THROUGH OTHERS

To be successful as a leader, spend as much time as possible helping others become successful. Look at the work of most great leaders, and you'll see that they view themselves primarily as support people. Their job is to work for the people who report to them; doing everything they can to help be as productive as possible. In his book, *The Contrarian's Guide to Leadership*, Dr. Steven Sample contends that a leader should spend 10 percent of his/her time hiring, firing, evaluating, and motivating; and the remaining 90 percent clearing obstacles and providing resources to those that work for and with him/her.

THE MIND-BODY CONNECTION IN LEARNING

A lot of what's going on in management trends has to do with learning, whether it's individual, team based, or organizational. Researchers are documenting the relationship between the mind and body for the importance of receptivity and promotion of learning. What does all this mean to you? They've established a mind-body connection to learning. To be a better learner, you must also be aware of how you care for, feed, and exercise your body and brain. Here are some suggestions to keep you at optimal performance:

- Feed your brain. It's the hungriest organ, consuming 25 percent of the daily intake of glucose. To ensure it doesn't go hungry, feed it plenty of complex carbohydrates, fats, and proteins at all meals but especially at midday (that doesn't mean bust your diet).
- Physical exercise provides a great boost to mental performance, but it's not enough. You have to exercise mentally. Challenging mental tasks keep your synaptic pathways alive even as you age. (And boy, do I need to keep mine alive?)

BOOST YOUR MEMORY

If you feel stressed at work and are having trouble remembering things, here are some suggestions to boost your memory (according to Cynthia Green, PhD, Mt. Sinai School of Medicine):

- Exercise regularly. People who are aerobically fit have the best memories.
- Get enough rest. Being tired makes it harder to access information stored in memory. Sleep needs vary by person, so get enough sleep each night that you feel rested and alert.

NO TRADING PLACES

They may make more money than us and they may drive us crazy (sometimes), but we don't want to trade places with them. Who is it? Your boss! Every year, the Marlin Company and Harris Interactive conduct a survey to explore workers' opinions in an array of job-related subjects. According to a recent workplace attitudes survey, 73 percent of American workers said they would not want their boss's job. Increased stress and alienation were cited as two reasons for not wanting the increased responsibility. How do you feel about this? Do you want to move up to your boss's position, or are you comfortable with what you have now? Take a few minutes to think about what your boss really does. Can you deal with the added stress, the meetings, the constant policy changes, limited resources, vacancies that go unfilled for long periods of time, etc? Is it really worth the hassle? Hey, one of these days you may have to make that decision. Will you be ready to do it without reservations?

DON'T ISOLATE YOURSELF AT WORK

According to Mel Silberman, PhD, president of Princeton, New Jersey – based Active Training, the importance of being a team player in today's work environment can't be overestimated. It's essential that workers don't isolate themselves in their jobs. Team players have the ability to blend their talents with the skills of others around them. They balance interest in what they are advocating with interests in what others are saying. Team players see themselves and others as group resources rather than individual egos. Dr. Silberman says, *"Team players act as if they are part of the group's pool of knowledge, skills and ideas and are successful in getting others to act that way themselves."*

RESOLVE CONFLICTS AT WORK IMMEDIATELY

Resolving conflicts at work can be extremely tricky, particularly if you find it difficult to be confrontational. Many people would rather walk away from a dispute, but prolonging a problem can only make matters worse in the long run. Here are some suggestions to help you deal with disagreements:

- Be able to confront disagreements without being disagreeable.
- Get at the root of the problem by putting the real issues on the table, then work to negotiate win-win situations.
- Never walk around holding in your resentments. Find a way to deal with conflicts within one to two days.
- Don't be on the defensive. Listen with compassion to what your coworkers have to say.

TOO MUCH PAPER

Are you overwhelmed with paper? Whatever happened to the promise of the electronic age to produce a paperless society? Despite computers and other electronic devices, it's estimated that at least 90 percent of the world's information still resides on paper. And paper often equates to clutter. Time management experts insist that clutter amounts to postponed decisions. So how can you reduce the clutter in your office to become more effective and productive? Get rid of the clutter. Be merciless – throw away all unnecessary paper and reports. To decide what information to keep, focus on your organization's mission and goals. Think about what information will support your work to reach those goals and objectives. Dump anything that isn't pertinent, or if you're hesitant or afraid to dispose of something that may be important later on, store the material in a centralized storage system that's well labeled for accessibility.

SICK LEAVE IS USED FOR MANY REASONS

What are you using your sick leave for? According to a survey of personnel offices in 333 U.S. companies, more people are using sick leave for family and personal reasons than for illness. About one-third of unscheduled days off are because of sickness. The rest are used to deal with family issues, stress, and personal needs. The survey found that the rate of unscheduled absences has remained the same for years. However, unscheduled absences for family issues increased from 20 percent in 2000 to 28 percent in 2006, and absences due to stress jumped from 5 percent to 19 percent for the same period. For some federal employees, sick leave is money in the bank. For others, it's the hedge on catastrophic illness or injury rather than use-or-lose sick leave as many consider it. It's a valuable benefit and should be used wisely.

RETURNING SICK/INJURED WORKERS TO WORK SOONER

Instead of keeping people home until they're fully recovered, federal programs mandate that agencies try to put sick or injured workers back to work as soon as feasible. Oftentimes they are returned to light duty jobs with fewer work hours or less demanding work requirements. If done right, workers keep an attachment to their jobs, and the agency reduces sick leave or worker's compensation costs. An industry survey by Mercer Human Resources Consulting found an average worker's compensation claim loss of $2.08 for each $100 of payroll in 2003, up about 25 percent over 2000; and the year wasn't over yet. If mission needs aren't a legitimate-enough reason, this should be sufficient motivation for managers to work to get people back on the job ASAP.

CHOOSE YOU WORDS CAREFULLY

An important part of communication is your choice of words. Here are some classes of words that you should use carefully:

- **Jargon** – the technical language you use in your profession. Jargon is confusing for those who don't use it often. When using jargon with outsiders, you won't be considered more intelligent, just inconsiderate and out of touch.
- **Idioms** – the language particular to a certain people or area. While it may be entertaining in some situations, in a professional context, if you can't be understood or if you sound too colloquial, people may lower their opinion of you.

LANGUAGE DEFINES YOU

If you're concerned about the image you're projecting on the job, be aware of your language. It's not just off-color language that's problematic. Image consultants advise that the use of slang and jargon should be avoided. Think about your use of grammar. Is it proper, or could you use a refresher course? Well-spoken employees are considered more professional and, therefore, more likely to be considered valuable and more likely to be promoted.

K-I-S-S YOUR RESUME?

Something I've relearned" recently. When writing a resume, follow the K-I-S-S rule: keep it short and specific. If you include a career objective, it should be simple and to the point. Place the main focus on your skills and experience. Keep the information succinct and specific. More and more, managers are looking for people with specific skills to perform specific tasks rather than people who can fill job titles. The more information you can convey about your skills, the better your chances of getting that next job – the one you've been working toward.

EFFECTIVE COMMUNICATING

Many of the problems that occur in an organization are the direct result of people failing to communicate (as if you didn't already know that). Faulty communication, the kind that is an honest attempt but comes out garbled or incoherent, causes the most problems. Effective communication, the other kind, occurs only if the receiver understands the exact information or idea that the sender intended to transmit. It's a matter of teamwork. Many leaders think they have communicated once they've told a team member to do something. However, a message has *not* been communicated unless it is fully understood by the receiver. If you want to know if someone got the message, ask for feedback. Feedback tells the sender that the receiver understood the message, its level of importance, and what must be done with it. Communication, then, is an exchange, not just a give. All the players must participate to complete the information exchange.

GET DUMPED ON

Encourage people to dump on you! Welcome people to share their issues and concerns. If you're not hearing about problems, it means you're out of touch and need to find out what's going on. Pronto! Have weekly right-or-wrong discussions. Schedule time to discuss what went right and why, as well as what went wrong. When you lay things out on the table for discussion, you create an opportunity to learn from one another and do better the next time. A good listener is not only popular, but after a while he even knows something as well.

PROVIDE THE SPARK

A big part of a leader's job is to provide the energy for the organization. Leaders are the batteries that jump-start people and get individuals and teams moving. Along the way, they also act as cheerleaders to keep energy levels up. But getting and keeping people excited about their jobs, enthused about the team, and motivated about what they can accomplish is not easy.

Some techniques that help provide the spark are:

- Encourage people to meet and mingle. Help them to really get to know.
- Create a culture of creativity by showing people that you want and value their ideas. Ideas are the lifeblood of the organization.
- Develop and practice contagious enthusiasm. When they see you excited about a project, they get excited too.
- Work hard, play hard. Working hard demonstrates commitment, but a good leader also values play. After reaching a difficult goal or completing a big project, ease the pressure.
- Give people time to relax and savor the quality of their work.

THE FIVE As OF LEADERSHIP:

- **Approachable:** Listen to what others have to say. Make yourself accessible – listen to what they have to say. You may learn something.
- **Accepting:** Keep an open mind. Good ideas can come from anywhere. In fact, many of the best ideas come from the line workers – they understand what's going on and how the process works.
- **Acknowledging:** Recognize the contributions of others. Thank someone every day and let them know they've done a good job.
- **Accountable:** Be responsible for yourself and the actions of your subordinates. Never say "it's not my fault."
- **Adaptable:** Change is not so much an aspect of the business as it is the business itself. In the R&D (test and evaluation) business, if nothing changes, you may be out of work. Change is good, necessary, and inevitable. Think about where your organization and your people need to be in the future, not where you are today, and make the adjustments necessary to get there.

THE *IRE* OF LEADERSHIP

- **DESIRE** a better way.
- **INQUIRE** into facts and findings.
- **PERSPIRE** often and a lot.
- **ADMIRE** other's accomplishments.
- **INSPIRE** the people around you.
- **REQUIRE** effort and results.

"Leadership is the art of getting someone to do what you want done because he or she wants to do it." (Dwight D. Eisenhower)

DIFFERENCES

People ask the difference between a leader and a boss. Teddy Roosevelt said, "The leader works in the open and the boss in covert. The leader leads, and the boss drives." More precisely:

- The boss drives people; the leader coaches them.
- The boss depends on authority; the leader on good will.
- The boss inspires fear; the leader enthusiasm.
- The boss says "I"; the leader says "We."
- The boss fixes blame for the problem; the leader fixes the problem.
- The boss says, "Go"; the leader says, "Let's go!"

THE THREE MOST IMPORTANT WORDS IN LEADERSHIP: *COMMUNICATE, COMMUNICATE, AND COMMUNICATE*

Remember: True communication involves the participation of two or more individuals in speaking, listening, and acting to satisfy each other's goals.

Map your communication plan:

- Establish the vision – show people where you want to go
- Articulate the strategies – tell them how to get there
- Identify benchmark achievement – show how they will know they are on the way, and
- Provide a flexible method for continuous feedback – ask for input during the journey.

MORE COMMUNICATION

Assume nothing; Teach everything. Good leaders prepare people and provide them with the tools and resources they need to succeed.

Go out and make regular contact. Don't make them come to you.

Get personal! Relate your personal experience (mistakes, nice tries, and successes). Most people find leaders who share something of themselves to be more credible than those who don't.

"Start with the premise that the function of leadership is to produce more leaders, not more followers." (Ralph Nader)

LEADERSHIP DEVELOPMENT

If you were to list the attributes of the best leaders you've known, chances are that list would include "helping others to grow and develop." Somewhere, at some time, you probably had a leader who helped you do just that! However, before you can lead others, you must learn to lead yourself. You have to know yourself. If you're secure in your beliefs, others will follow. As such, leaders spend time developing people for the same reason coaches spend time developing players: they understand that the strength of the organization lies in the talents of its people. Some call this collective talent "intellectual capital." Leaders know they have a responsibility to grow this capital so that it pays dividends to the organization.

DEVELOP YOURSELF AND OTHERS

How do you get human capital to pay dividends through individual and team development? Leaders enhance the talents and skills of their people and prepare them to be the leaders of tomorrow. Some ideas for improving and developing yourself and others:

- **DRESS FOR LEADERSHIP.** Seriously. Even in the age of business casual, the way you dress influences other people's perceptions of you. As a rule of thumb, dress one level above the people you're leading.
- **GET RID OF CLUTTER!** Keep your desk or work area orderly. It needn't look like a photo op, but if it's always a mess, it won't inspire confidence in others.
- **SHARPEN YOUR SOCIAL SKILLS.** Have you ever worked with someone who was very smart, but you couldn't stand him because he was a pain in the butt? It may be trite but true. People don't care how much you know, until they know how much you care.

- **BE COURTEOUS!** Like Grandma told you, if you're nice to others, they'll be nice to you. Greet people warmly. Shake hands as if you mean it; look them in the eye and grasp their hand firmly.
- **THINK!** Once upon a time, a long time ago when I was a kid, that was the mantra of IBM. It was posted on the wall of every classroom, elementary through high school where I come from. It means taking time to consider the situation and the consequences of a decision before you act. Try it sometime. You may find it works.
- **Know thyself!** Get in the habit of examining your beliefs and behaviors. None of us is perfect (some nearly); none of us is all bad. Somewhere in the middle is the real *us*. Self-awareness is critical to being an effective leader.
- **Trust in your values**. Believe in yourself. If you're in a leadership position, it's likely you got there because you're a good and decent person with an inner compass that usually points you in the right direction.
- A leader must **be driven by vision,** but be willing to nurture the talents and ideas of others. Be smart enough to run with a good idea no matter who originated it. *That's leadership!*

Leadership is rooted in character (I know, we have plenty of characters). Some of the attributes of character and their practice are:

- **Be responsible!** Responsibility means a willingness to be accountable for the actions of others as well as your personal actions. (Isn't responsibility the foundation for all leadership behaviors?)
- **Be honest.** By telling the truth you establish trust and a sense of faith – if you screw up and admit it, people deal with it much better. Making mistakes is part of living. The trick is to minimize the impact of the mistakes and the number you make.
- **Practice wisdom.** It's essential that leaders maintain an outlook that measures future vision against the reality of the current situation. Wisdom comes from experience and the flexibility to reevaluate.
- **Leadership takes guts.** Show a willingness to take a stand on unpopular decisions or uncomfortable issues. You don't have to always agree, but you always have to comply.

Hey! Is it getting to be that time of year when you should be thinking about performance appraisals? If you're doing your job as a supervisor and leader, you'll be concentrating on the performance of your employees and your goals for the organization.

- **Tell others what you *expect*!** They need to know exactly what you want. The position description is not a task list; so it doesn't describe everything you want and expect.
- **Focus on performance.** Just because you don't like someone's taste in clothes, music, or hair doesn't mean they're not doing a good job. Encourage them to be who they are.
- **Level the playing field.** When your expectations are clear, everyone has an equal chance to succeed. Soon you'll know who wants to do well, and who doesn't give a darn. Reward the achievers; challenge the slackers.

WHAT *INEFFECTIVE* LEADERS HAVE TO SAY

"Because I said so!"

"Of course I want you to take risks. Just don't make any mistakes!"

"Hey, don't blame me. This wasn't my idea."

"Don't ask questions – just do what you're told."

"If I wanted your opinion, I would have asked for it!"

"Handle this – just don't make any decisions."

"I don't owe you any explanation!"

"You're not paid to think. You're paid to do your job."

"It's my way or the highway!"

"So what if I said that yesterday? This is today!"

"It's my job to make the decisions and your job to carry them out."

"Why can't you be like everyone else?"

"Someday you'll be in charge, and then it'll be your turn to tell people what to do."

If you're ever tempted to say any of these, *fight the feeling*!

EMPOWER OTHERS TO LEAD

One of the most common mistakes managers make is assuming too much authority. As a result, they quickly become buried under a mountain of work, and they either quit or burn out. They fail to learn a key lesson of leadership: *the more control you relinquish, the more you retain.* Delegation of responsibility not only shares the workload, but it also extends the boundaries of authority.

The role of a leader is to create vision, set expectations, and lead by example. But leaders also determine the course of action for others to follow. That involves allowing others to participate by setting their own expectations and determining their own example by which to lead. This is called *"empowerment."*

When people feel they have responsibility, they're more likely to take ownership of the process. They become more accountable, and they care about the results. These are the kinds of people you need. Why? Because they manage themselves under the general direction of *a leader who trusts them to do what is right for the job and for the organization.*

EMPOWERMENT AS A TOOL

Delegate responsibility and authority. Assign a big job to one of your more promising team members. Encourage him/her to develop a work plan, make decisions, solve problems, and be accountable for results. The leader who takes control over a problem gets the right people to solve it and supports them is the type of person that organizations need most.

Be a good sales person. "Salesmanship" is the ability to persuade others of the benefits of a good idea. One of the roles of the leader is persuading others to act in certain ways. Remember, good salesmanship results in the recipient feeling good about his/her decision. In other words, effective leadership enriches both leader and follower.

Push decision making to the front lines. Frontline decision-making leads to frontline leadership.

Empower yourself! Don't wait for the title of leader before you act as one.

Everyone has an invisible sign hanging from his or her neck saying, "Make me feel important."

- **Decide who should decide.** Every time you face a decision, ask yourself: "Should I be doing this, or can it be done just as well, or even better, by one of my team members?" Some of the best-run organizations are those that run themselves – those in which decision making happens at all levels.
- **Focus on results.** Tell others what you expect. Then provide all the necessary resources and make sure they have the authority and the support to do what they need to do. Then you can hold them accountable.
- **Don't hoard information – share it.** Studies show that when people know what's going on, they better understand their roles and what they need to do.
- **Ask others to help you identify obstacles to effective leadership.** Is it them? Is it you? Is it the system? Get ideas for removing these obstacles and then do what you can to eliminate them (the obstacles).

ASK OTHERS TO "DRIVE FOR A WHILE"

Empower others to lead by encouraging them to step forward and assume leadership roles. Do you know someone in your organization that would make a good leader? Challenge them to step forward, give them a little nudge, and cheer them on.

Foster and encourage cooperation.

Get rid of the "my way or the highway" mentality. Sometimes the best course of action for an organization is to tolerate and even encourage dissent.

Give ownership of a problem to those who must implement the solution.

Provide guidance, but leave the details to them. Trust them to do their jobs. At the same time, stay in the loop. Be available for support and stay informed of progress.

MAKIN' A LIST AND CHECKIN' IT TWICE

- Make a list of people who could do some or all of your job. Let them know how you feel about their abilities and see what you can do to help them prepare for leadership.

- Occasionally, make yourself unavailable and inaccessible. Let people know that when you're gone, you expect them to assume responsibility and make decisions. *Then get lost!*
- **BECOME A PLAYER'S COACH**! Okay. I know it's an overused metaphor, but maybe that's because it fits! Think about it. Coaches who are respected by their teams instill in their players a purpose to win. Good coaches put their players in a position where they will play their best; they help players meld their individual sense of purpose with that of the team. That's a recipe for success in any organization.
- **Know when to back off**. Leaders need to have a physical presence so that followers will know who they are, but a leader also needs to learn when to back off. Too much presence stifles the group's ability to work things out for themselves limiting their ability to grow.
- Make sure you **always align team goals to organizational goals**. In other words, get everyone singing from the same sheet of music.

RECOGNIZE ACHIEVEMENT

Think about your own situation. How do you feel when you're recognized for something you've accomplished? Chances are you feel real good. You're not alone. Research shows that a key reason – sometimes the biggest reason – that people work is to feel appreciated. However, in the hustle and bustle of trying to get things done, we often forget to show appreciation to the people who work with us and do a good job every day. It's no wonder it's hard to keep some people.

The good news is that recognition isn't only simple, but it's also easy. In fact, of all the leadership behaviors, it's the easiest to do. So how can you start the recognition habit? With two simple words: *thank you.*

THANKS

When we say thank-you, we show that we value the other person's effort, and we appreciate the time and energy invested. And guess what? Saying thank-you often creates a culture of recognition in which people go out of their way to appreciate their coworkers' efforts. What else? When people feel recognized, they tend to contribute more. Studies show that they inspire others to follow their example. Soon you have an organization of inspired, motivated, and excited individuals that look forward to coming to work. Imagine that! Not hating your job, what a novel concept.

INSPIRED, MOTIVATED, AND EXCITED

How do we make this happen? Here are some ideas:

- Good ideas, like good people, need to be noticed. Let people know what you think of their ideas. They need to know you value their input. Don't assume that they know you appreciate them or their ideas.
- Remember that recognition is critical to self-esteem. Without it, we feel undervalued, even insignificant. Sometimes a simple pat on the back will go a long way toward making someone feel valued.
- Recognize someone's good work in front of their peers. You know the old adage, "Praise in public, punish in private." But . . .
- Be sensitive to people who don't like fusses made over them in public. There are a few who say, "Save the public recognition for the young guys or gals who need those kinds of things to enhance their careers, don't waste them on us old guys." (Guess who).

Make a list of what each person in your section wants most: more responsibility, more decision-making authority, less administrivia, etc. Refer to it whenever you're planning change. Helping others reach their career goals is a powerful form of recognition.

Make a habit of saying "I appreciate the work you do," but be sure to give specific feedback on what they did that was good.

Champion your staff to your customers. Let them know how much you value people. When customers see that kind of culture, it makes them feel good about doing business with you and your organization.

GIVE PEOPLE OPTIONS

- If you have an employee who wants to move up in the organization, put him or her in a position to do that. If you have an employee who wants to spend more time at home, consider flexible ways to provide it.
- Remember that people marry people, not organizations! Recognize that your people have another life. No matter how enthusiastic and committed they are to their jobs, they do have a family. Allow them time for family needs. Annual leave, sick leave, alternative work schedules are all designed to enhance family time and activities.
- Give your people IOUs. When they do something great, ask how they would like to be rewarded. Then, do what they requested at the first opportunity – assuming, of course, that it's reasonable and appropriate.

CLOSING THOUGHTS
(well, almost)

You really want to get someone's attention? *Share success!* When people do an exceptional job, mail a note to their family letting them know how special you think they are. Wouldn't that blow their minds?

Finally, *so what makes a good leader?* There are many attributes and characteristics found in effective leaders. But one thing's for certain: Regardless of the leadership characteristic, intention alone isn't good enough. You have to walk the talk. After all, it's how you actually behave that ultimately defines your success and determines how you will be judged as a leader.

Pete Smith, CEO of the Private Sector Council, a nonprofit group working to improve federal management practices, addressed the American Society of Public Administration in a recent speech and emphasized the failure of government to make leadership skills training and application a priority.

He said, leaders exist at all levels of an organization, not just at the top, and should be fully assimilated into the management process, an important aspect in the current culture of teamwork. He noted that there is no secret formula for leadership and that there are seventy-six thousand books on the subject at Amazon.com, including reviews of the leadership skills of Attila the Hun and Mother Teresa (now there's a combination).

He went on to point out those top-notch leaders "have a genuine, deep concern for an important, worthwhile mission and the vision is so strong that it can easily be felt by others. It's tangible, it's exciting, and it draws people in." (I don't want to say I told you so but . . .)

Leaders know that the mission is more important than they are, and great leaders do not abuse their positions. "In fact," he said, "most of them greatly enjoy interacting with the rank and file, being where the real work is done." He claimed that corporations and governments have not done a good enough job of growing such leaders and that, with few exceptions, leadership development is not integral to the executive culture.

Therefore, he said, current career leaders have a responsibility "to help employees and their *new* [italics mine] leaders understand the value of change, to capture progress made and to keep things moving forward." In other words, once you become a leader (just because you become one doesn't mean you are one!), leadership doesn't stop. If anything, it becomes more demanding; there is a greater need for learning, experiencing, and practicing the art of leadership. Also among those demands is the development of new leaders to ultimately replace those getting ready to check out.

According to a study by the U.S. Office of Personnel Management, *good employees* – those demonstrating mastery of the technical aspects of their jobs – tend to be rewarded with promotions into managerial positions where responsibility for decisions rise and where, to be effective, managers need to have at least a basic understanding of the nuances of the operation, not just the overall picture. I've been saying it for forty years!

Actually I've said we promote people into managerial/supervisory positions for all the wrong reasons. We promote them because they're good technicians, not because they're good supervisors or managers or because they have some special aptitude that makes them good supervisory candidates. Those skills have to be developed. They don't automatically come with the promotion, and for some, they never come.

Recent surveys have validated what I've said. Employees complain that middle managers, promoted for their skills as employees, remain good employees, but never become good managers. They're promoted without regard to their leadership skills and are neither trained in nor rewarded for leadership competence once in those management positions.

To be an effective manager, one must essentially know the jobs of the employees below them and the executives above them. Sadly, top managers sometimes fail to recognize and fully utilize that knowledge and make matters worse by not allowing managers to lead or to make decisions even though they may have selected the individual for the manager position. Top leaders quickly learn that they can count on managers, so they tend to use them much as personal staff rather than leaders of organizations.

People emulate their superiors. Leaders who expect their managers to be leaders must also show leadership, signaling that managing people matters; that includes writing performance evaluations, making recommendations for awards based on real performance, and making promotion selections based on technical competence. If leaders exhibit little interest in sound people management, the problem is perpetuated.

Managers answering the surveys said they could use a little slack in the rules and procedures. They often must get approval for the most mundane tasks and multiple sign-offs from above for trivial matters, i.e., routine personnel decisions and minor operational choices.

Generally, managers are very good. They're chosen because they're, allegedly, the best at what they do, dedicated to the mission, the most productive, trusted, and technically competent. However, expectations for them often become overwhelmed by the constraints placed on them by the leadership. When this happens, they simply take the easy way and ride it out till retirement (or are promoted beyond their level of competence).

Beware the pitfalls of new leadership positions.

(Taken from: Michael Watkins, *The First 90 Days: Critical Success Strategies for New Leaders at All Levels*, [HBS Press, 2003])

Every few thousand years employees who've been good technical worker bees enter supervisory/managerial positions, often technically ill-equipped for the task. Their actions, or lack thereof, during the first few months can determine their success or failure, yet little advice is available on how to take charge in a new managerial role. These transition periods are critical because of the vulnerability of new leaders who lack detailed knowledge of their newly acquired roles.

SEVEN COMMON TRAPS FOR LEADERS

- **BEING ISOLATED**
  Relying on reports and analysis rather than devoting time to meet and talk with new colleagues can isolate new leaders. The need to know an organization before reforming it is often at the heart of the problem. If isolation continues too long, the leader is often labeled unapproachable. New leaders must get out and about in the organization quickly in order to gather impressions, ideas, and feelings about the work and the people and how to deal with issues and make crucial early decisions.

- **COMING IN WITH THE ANSWER**

  An all too common occurrence is the arrival of a leader with the answer – a fix for all of the organization's problems. Many fall into this trap through arrogance or insecurity. Others think they must be decisive to impress top management. Employees who see this and believe the leader's mind is made up are hesitant to share information or ideas, hindering the newcomer's ability to learn the true nature of the situation. New leaders must be willing to ask questions even if they're confident that they understand the problems and how to deal with them. The key is to take a systematic approach to problem solving and be efficient at learning and adopting methods/ideas for gaining the necessary insight into the organization and its mission.

- **STAYING TOO LONG WITH THE EXISTING TEAM**

  Many, especially those with respect for others, believe inherited subordinates deserve a chance to prove themselves. Some see it as an issue of fairness, others ignorance. Whatever the rationale, it's inadvisable to keep mediocre-performing team members. In the beginning, new leaders aren't held responsible for the team's performance, but that doesn't last long. Before long, the team is the leader's responsibility. Leaders are brought in to improve performance by initiating new ideas, making tough or unpopular decisions, and affecting a spirit of achievement. Keeping people who can't do the job wastes valuable time and energy. This doesn't mean that new leaders should be unfair, expect miracles, be arbitrary, or terminate people on the spot. They should make it clear, however, that there is a time limit for deciding who's going to be in the game when the whistle blows. Personnel adjustments, to include removal, may be daunting, but not impossible, and the effort is usually worth it.

- **ATTEMPTING TOO MUCH**

  Some try to do too many things at once. It's application of the theory, "If I get enough things going, something is bound to work." These kinds of leaders are sending the message that winners are proactive and able to handle diverse challenges simultaneously. This is both confusing and overwhelming to the organization. Given the many demands on organizations, the risk of overload is great.

The root of this pitfall often lies in a lack of prioritizing or poor planning on the part of the leader. Early on, leaders must identify the few top priorities then discipline themselves and the organization to focus on those priorities.

- **BEING CAPTURED BY THE WRONG PEOPLE**
  The arrival of a new leader inevitably leads to jockeying for position in the new "regime" by those who had influence in the old one. Among the people vying for attention will be those who are incapable, well-meaning but out of touch, intent on misleading, or in search of power for power's sake. New leaders must exercise caution in deciding who to listen to and to what degree. Advisors that don't represent a broad group of people have skewed or limited information, or use their proximity to the leader to push private agendas alienate others and close off valuable input.

  Whether from the outside or promoted from within, new leaders must keep lines of communication open to balance internal influence. Just as you are known by the company you keep, judgments about new leaders are based on perceptions of who influences them.

- **SETTING UNREALISTIC EXPECTATIONS**
  Managing expectations begins the moment a new leader arrives on the job. For those hired from the outside, it begins sooner, during the job interview. It's easy to set unrealistic expectations about what can be accomplished. New leaders want to impress, and new bosses often expect miracles. Performance expectations are typically determined early before the new leader has a thorough understanding of the situation.

  New leaders should never presume that their initial situational analysis will or should remain unchanged. They should devote considerable effort to dialogue with their superiors and other key persons.

- **FAILING TO BUILD COALITIONS**
  Many new leaders devote too much time during start-up to the vertical dimensions of influence – upward to bosses and downward to subordinates – and not enough to the horizontal dimension of peers and key external associates. This is understandable since leaders naturally gravitate to the people they report to and who report to them. But sooner or later (probably sooner), new leaders need the support of people who aren't under their authority.

  Building coalitions is especially critical for leaders. They must identify who influences key decisions and what they care about and who influences the influencers. Then they need to craft a plan to reach out and build support.

Avoiding these traps depends on how well new leaders prepare for and manage their transition from worker to leader. This means carefully diagnosing situations, identifying personal vulnerabilities, accelerating their learning, negotiating success, building coalitions, and winning early victories.

At some time recently, I used the term "emotional intelligence." What does it mean to the average person trying to improve his/her status in the workforce? I'll try to explain it in as concise a way as I can yet capture the essence of what I'm talking about.

SELF-AWARENESS

High self-awareness refers to having an accurate understanding of how you behave, how other people perceive you; recognizing how you respond to others; being sensitive to your attitudes, feelings, emotions, intentions, and general communication style at *any given moment* and being able to accurately express this awareness to others.

SKILL INDICATORS

- Know when you're thinking negatively.
- Know when talking to yourself is helpful.
- Know when you're becoming angry.
- Know how you're interpreting events.
- Know what senses you're currently using.
- Know how to communicate accurately what you experience.
- Know the moments your mood shifts.
- Know when you're becoming defensive.
- Know the impact your behavior has on others.
- Able to identify shifts in physiological arousal.
- Be able to relax in pressure situations.
- Act productively in anxiety-arousing situations.
- Calm oneself quickly when angry.
- Associate different physiological cues with different emotional states.
- Use self-talk to affect emotional states.
- Communicate feelings effectively.
- Reflect on negative feelings without being distressed.
- Stay calm when you're the target of anger from others.
- Be aqble to gear up at will.
- Be able to regroup quickly after a setback.

- Be able to complete long-term tasks in designated time frames.
- Be able to produce high energy in the context of low-enjoyment work.
- Be able to change and stop ineffective habits.
- Be able to develop new and productive patterns of behavior.
- Be able to follow through words with actions.

SKILLS ASSESSMENT

- Do you recognize your feelings and emotions as they happen?
- Are you aware of how others perceive you?
- How do you act when you're defensive?
- Do you use anger productively?
- Can you manage your anxiety in times of change?
- Are you aware of how you speak to yourself?
- Can you put yourself in a good mood?
- Are you persistent?
- Do setbacks set you back?
- Can you psyche yourself up?

MANAGING EMOTIONS

The capacity to comfort yourself, to shake off rampant anxiety, gloom, despair, or irritability is managing your emotions. It's also the ability to keep an emotional perspective.

MOTIVATION

Be able to channel emotions to achieve a goal; to postpone immediate gratification for future gratification; to be productive in low interest, low enjoyment activities; to persist in the face of frustration and generate initiative without external pressure.

EMPATHY

When you're empathetic, you have the ability to exchange information on a meaningful level. You're also adept in skills necessary for organizing groups and building teams, negotiating solutions, mediating conflict among others, building consensus, and making personal connections.

SOCIAL SKILLS

Being aware of other people's feelings and emotions; being able to listen to their feelings; being able to help others deal with their feelings and emotions in productive ways and assist them in increasing their awareness about their own impact on others.

MANAGEMENT LESSONS FOR THOSE WHO WOULD BE BOSS:

ENVISION YOURSELF AS BOSS

To get ahead in your career, start thinking of yourself as a successful executive. According to the president of the Duncan Group, workers should see themselves as the largest shareholder of their own business. Todd Duncan encourages workers to adopt a CEO mind-set. He says that the most successful people buy stock in themselves. Duncan advises you to stop thinking of yourself as an employee with a job and start thinking of yourself as an owner of a business with a compelling vision to help people. This is a key to success whether in the private or public sector. We, in the organization, are here to provide a service to customers (within the limits of the law). How well we do that is reflected in how others see us and in the respect we get. If we get no respect, we should be asking ourselves why. The test and evaluation function, for example, is our business – we own it! We're the ones that make it go. Therefore, we should take pride in how well we run it.

Lesson No. 1:

An eagle was sitting on a tree resting, doing nothing.

A small rabbit saw the eagle and asked him, "Can I also sit like you and do nothing?"

The eagle answered: "Sure, why not." So the rabbit sat on the ground below the eagle and rested.

All of a sudden, a fox appeared, jumped on the rabbit and ate it.

Management moral – to be sitting and doing nothing, you must be sitting very, very high up.

Lesson No. 2:

A turkey was chatting with a bull. "I would love to be able to get to the top of that tree," sighed the turkey, "but I haven't got the energy."

"Well, why don't you nibble on some of my droppings?" replied the bull. "They're packed with nutrients."

The turkey pecked at a lump of dung and found it actually gave him enough strength to reach the lowest branch of the tree. The next day, after eating some more dung, he reached the second branch. Finally after a fourth night, the turkey was proudly perched at the top of the tree.

He was promptly spotted by a farmer who shot him out of the tree.

Management moral/lesson – bull shit might get you to the top, but it won't keep you there.

Lesson No. 3:

A little bird was flying south for the winter. It was so cold that the bird froze and fell to the ground into a large field.

While he was lying there, a cow came by and dropped some dung on him. As the frozen bird lay there in the pile of cow dung, he began to realize how warm he was. The dung was actually thawing him out! He lay there all warm and happy and soon began to sing for joy.

A passing cat heard the bird singing and came to investigate. Following the sound, the cat discovered the bird under the pile of cow dung and promptly dug him out and ate him.

Management moral/lessons:

1. Not everyone who shits on you is your enemy.
2. Not everyone who gets you out of shit is your friend.
3. And when you're in deep shit, it's best to keep your mouth shut!

This ends your two-minute management course!

Traditionally, we've been taught that people learn to lead by progressing through successive levels of expertise in an organizational stovepipe. However, one compelling counterargument claims this idea is clearly the wrong way to develop successful leaders as is the assumption that something magical happens when people attend an expensive and renowned training program. These are myths and they're expensive myths.

In short, to help beginning employees learn to lead, an organization needs to intentionally adopt an approach to providing a variety of challenging job experiences such as job rotations; having senior leaders walk alongside them as coaches, teachers, and mentors; letting them watch senior leaders themselves lead by example; and then, spending some time in reflection with them so that learning can be further embedded when some of the inevitable failures occur. This is called a culture change, but because of the demands of the mission, it doesn't happen very often.

This approach to development, then, must become not so much a program as a way of life. In the best organizations, leaders take the time to help younger potential leaders learn by experience, who in turn help those behind them learn to lead. This is servant leadership in action. Once you have three generations of leaders, you'll know you have embedded the practice into the culture. That's an investment of time that's well worth the lessons learned – and it's an investment that leaves a legacy.

A recent report published by the Center for Creative Leadership offers several specific ways to increase the leadership potential of staff managers. I'll try to summarize their conclusions.

1. Evaluate Staff Professionals for Management Potential and Intent Early

Although many staff professionals prefer to remain individual contributors, it's not true that most would rather be workers than managers or couldn't make better managers if given proper preparation and opportunity. Success isn't so much based on where or how one started as it is based on one's later experiences.

Early identification of those staff contributors who show signs of managerial and leadership potential and interest is the first step toward providing them with opportunities for leadership challenges. Although most staff professionals are evaluated early, these evaluations generally concentrate on technical rather than leadership and management skills.

2. Ration Development Jobs Carefully

Because supervisory roles are key sources for learning leadership skills and because they are scarcer in staff units (which are flatter than line units), these positions should be reserved for staff who are identified early as showing a potential for management.

3. Enrich (Provide More Variety in) the Leadership Experience of Staff Managers

When making managerial assignments, leaders must think in terms of a transition from one type of challenge to another. Managers develop most when leadership demands change – for instance, when they have to work with new people or technologies or develop a new skill – and they must give up the old, familiar ways of getting the job done.

Leaders should ask themselves the questions, "What will this person have to learn quickly? What will the person have to unlearn, give up doing, or change?" In other words, when placing an individual in one of two possible staff assignments, choose the one that offers the most change, thereby providing diversity and variety for the developing individual. That strategy will provide the opportunity to develop resourcefulness and the capacity to learn in a hurry, two important leadership skills.

4. Think Small

There are a limited number of high-challenge jobs in any organization, and they should be rationed carefully. In addition, many mini-opportunities exist: organizing an off-site meeting or developing a new training program; working with a problem subordinate; handling personnel or morale problems, cutting costs, or streamlining operations; giving someone a stretch project assignment. These can all teach how to develop others and involve working with those not worked with before.

5. Use the Principle of Progression

Successful managers had chains of small but progressively more challenging opportunities as they developed. These opportunities are available in most staff organizations.

6. Provide Lots of Career Information and Feedback to All Staff Managers and Professionals

In order to take an active part in their own development, staff professionals need three things: an understanding of how the organization defines effectiveness and success (and ineffectiveness and derailment); a knowledge of what experience (in terms of jobs and job challenges) can lead to the competencies that constitute effectiveness; and frequent and varied feedback on their progress in attaining these competencies. The first two are sometimes problematic. Oftentimes, the success measures of organizations are wish lists of desirable values and characteristics with no indication of where and how they can be attained. Discussions in which senior managers talk about their key experience and what they've learned can help, but nothing substitutes for a clear definition by the organization of what constitutes effectiveness and how it can be attained. The third is crucial. Staffers should receive multiple-perspective, 360-degree, actionable feedback (that is, from bosses, subordinates, peers, colleagues, customers, and so on) on their strengths and weaknesses; and this feedback should be received on a regular basis – not just during appraisal rating time.

7. Aggressively Help Staffers Learn from Each Experience

One of the main conclusions from the study is that successful people are active learners. For instance, they keep notes on interesting ideas, consolidate their learning through feedback or tutoring, or ask themselves probing questions: What am I learning? What do I need to do differently? What habits have become too comfortable for me? What do I need to do from a leadership perspective? Nevertheless, being an active listener isn't automatic. It's easy to go along, absorbed in your job, without reflecting on how you're acting, what the impact of your actions are, and whether your developing into a versatile manager able to cope with any leadership challenge. At a minimum, managers should consider their experiences and review new ones with developing subordinates.

8. Find Ways for Staffers to Be Involved in Worker-level Issues

There are numerous ways that staffers can be put to work on tough issues. Assign staff to work on resolving first-line problems. Arrange periodic workspace-oriented issue and problem reviews. Require them to work regularly with supervisors on urgent problems. The key idea is not to allow the staff to work isolated from the core business activity.

9. Urge Individual Staffers to Build Their Own Leadership Skills

Individual staff managers can take an active part in finding ways to promote their own development. They can be empowered to look for and volunteer for start-up or fix-it projects; define what constitutes effective leadership in their current positions and acquire feedback on how they are doing; seek out contacts with worker bees; take trips to field locations; or take part in committees on significant issues and problems. In order to do this, of course, they need to know what leadership competencies they need to develop and what experiences promote those competencies.

10. Expose Staffers to Customers

Staffers don't have as much contact with outside customers (nor as much exposure to the basic test functions) as those working in the field.

This isolation can be lessened by such measures as observing the work of test engineers/technicians, working with the customers for short periods of time, and visiting customers. Many organizations require managers and staff professionals to spend a week or two every year working in the field in order to better understand customers and the test business.

11. Look for Linelike Jobs in Staff Units

There are small linelike jobs in most staff areas. These have more direct measures of their effectiveness, tight repetitive time frames, and direct stand-alone decision-making on a daily basis than the usual staff job, and they often involve managing larger groups of people.

Examples are jobs in accounts payable and accounts receivable; jobs in tracking manning levels and updating UMD changes; or jobs managing the facilities and hardware in a resource management unit. It might be tough to get high-potential staffers to take such jobs since they often would rather plan, think, strategize, and influence than manage, direct, and oversee production. Some gentle persuasion might be required but these miniline jobs can help build leadership skills.

12. Look for Opportunities for Temporary Staff-to-line Switches

Staff-to-line switches are rare, but they should be used more frequently. They can be very beneficial because they provide staffers with a specific understanding of the leadership requirements of supervision. In general, such a switch should take place early in a career rather than late.

13. Look to Make Early Permanent Staff-to-line Transitions

Some staffers who show an early inclination toward management, and leadership should be moved into supervisory positions permanently as soon as possible. Look for likely transition points. Some organizations, in order to persuade people to take the chance, offer a "round-trip ticket" in case the transition doesn't work out.

14. Look to Experiences in Addition to Jobs

Because staff jobs and careers offer few leadership opportunities and the realities of business don't allow people to move around as much as is desirable, staffers can enhance their development by means of off-the-job projects and assignments – for instance, conferences, projects, committees, and special assignments.

15. Look to Outside-of-work Experiences

There are leadership challenges in church groups, community projects, charitable activities, and professional associations, and the staffer should be encouraged to make use of these developmental opportunities. (Besides, they look good on award recommendations).

16. Mix Line and Staff in Training and Development Programs

Where possible, training and development programs, whether internal or external, should include the participation of both supervisors and staff managers. Everyone would gain from this mixing strategy.

17.Use Line Supervisors on Temporary Staff Assignments as Special Mentors/Coaches for Staffers

First-line supervisors who are temporarily assigned to staff positions can be used as a developmental resource. They can be asked to coach one or more staff colleagues in line experiences and perspectives. They can act as presenters or discussion leaders in staff management development programs. They can attend meetings of staff units and provide a line outlook on the initiatives and program ideas under discussion.

18.Arrange for Staff Professionals to Attend Line Meetings and Off-sites

Often, first – or second-line supervisors hold meetings that exclude staff managers. It would be a useful developmental experience for staff managers to attend these meetings. Not only would the content of such programs be beneficial for staffers, but the chance to interact informally with line supervisors and field individuals would also help decrease the isolation that many staffers experience.

CONCLUSION

In examining the difference in leadership competencies between the staff managers and line supervisors, the study considered whether there might be explanations other than the differences in experience. Maybe the difference in managers could be traced to differences in people when they enter the organization. Perhaps people self-select into staff or supervisory careers based upon the precursors to leadership skills, with the more technically oriented going into staff and the leaders into supervision. However, there is no meaningful evidence of that. Researchers conclude that each person starts with the same foundation or characteristics for leadership competencies although they may differ in their beginning interests.

On the other hand, maybe managerial and supervisory jobs are different at the top. Perhaps staff jobs require less personal leadership and more technical expertise. If that's the case, developmental life for staff professionals would be all right because staff careers do build technical competence. Is it possible that staff executives don't need as much leadership competence? Studies have found that there are only small differences in degree between supervisory and staff roles, responsibilities, and jobs. The top jobs in both management and supervision have the same requirement for personal leadership; they are more similar than different.

Nevertheless, staff development can be improved. But there are real impediments, many of them structural, standing in the way of staff professionals who might develop into senior managers. The good news, however, is that this doesn't necessarily have to be the case. If senior leadership moves in an aggressive yet disciplined way to add diverse leadership challenges to the work of staff professionals and introduces these challenges early in their careers, the situation can change. The benefits of doing this are great: an increased pool of leaders for both supervisory and managerial functions; better leadership in staff units; and as an equal employment opportunity initiative, an increase in the number of women and minorities making it into senior management positions.

This subject came up in casual conversation as the path of development. The opinion of the parties was that in an age of touchy-feely consensus-building exercises, sometimes it's okay to be a tough guy.

Of course, it isn't good to be mean just for the sake of being mean. But studies have shown that the most successful ones are kind when they need to be and tough when they need to be. Smart leaders adapt their styles depending on the people they're dealing with, or the seriousness of the circumstances.

A confrontational, in-your-face style is a common leadership approach. For example, one leader may speak calmly to one subordinate but jump up and down, shouting at another. He/she may never lose control, but consciously uses aggressiveness when s/he thought it would help hold an employee accountable. Great bosses aren't necessarily aggressive, but they are rigorous.

One study claims the best leaders operate with a somewhat Socratic style, and use questions to gain understanding. For important decisions that rested entirely on them, they'd tend to ask lots of questions and examine the evidence, looking for the best answers, and then engineer what they believed to be the best decision for the organization. The goal was always to make the right decision happen, not necessarily to gain consensus.

One drawback to this style, however, is that managers can use it to bully employees into submission. The strongest leaders don't try to get everyone to agree with them. They try to get employees to come up with honest analysis and smart ideas.

The bottom line: you don't have to be the good guy all the time. But when you get tough, do it with the goal of motivating your employees to find the truth or get better results. And do it not out of anger, but out of a commitment to excellence.

1. Know Yourself

All leaders should be aware that they are, in fact, four or more people. They are who they are, and who they think they are, (and these are never the same); they are who their bosses think they are and who their subordinates think they are.

Leaders who work hard to get feedback from many sources are more likely to understand and control their various selves and, therefore, make better leaders.

2. Be Mentally Tough

Leaders must be brutally honest with themselves, or they'll slip into a habit of self-deception. Even the best leaders make mistakes. By ferreting out these mistakes and correcting them quickly, a good leader can become a great leader.

3. Be Magnanimous

Leaders who share their power and their time can accomplish extraordinary things. The best leaders understand that real leadership is the ability to free up talent. They gain power not only by giving it away, but also by not grabbing it back.

4. Listen Very Closely

The most important skill for leaders is listening. Introverts have a great edge since they tend to listen quietly and usually don't suffer from "interruptionism." Don't get caught up thinking about what you'll say next rather than hearing what's being said now.

5. Trust Your Instinct and Your Impulse

If something smells bad, sounds funny, or causes you to lose sleep at night, have chills, fever and nosebleeds, take another look. Your instincts combined with your experience can prevent you and your organization from blindly walking off a cliff.

6. Learn by Failure

Learn from your failures and become tolerant of the honest failure of others. When a setback comes along, try to treat it as a learning experience, for it will surely be that.

7. Beware of Certainty

Leaders should be a bit skeptical of anyone who is totally certain about their position. Leaders should have a reasonable doubt especially when dealing with true believers who are always sure they're right.

8. Be Decisive

The best leaders usually are forced to make prudent decisions when they only have about 60 percent of the information they need. Leaders who demand nearly all the information are usually months or years late making decisions.

9. Don't Become Indispensable

Organizations need indispensable foundations, not indispensable people. Leaders shouldn't allow themselves to become indispensable, nor should they let any of their subordinates become indispensable (or think they are).

10.Avoid the Tendency to Remain Silent

During meetings, oftentimes, we sit on our hands when it's time to raise an objection and speak up. Leadership requires the courage to make waves, to take on the bosses when they're wrong, and conviction.

11.Fight Paranoia

Welcome criticism; help people understand that it's okay to have issues with the organization. Loyalty and criticism are mutually supporting while captive loyalty is deadly. Avoid a defensive stance.

12.Be Goal Oriented

Leaders must try to set some long-term goals for their people and for their organization. People want to know where they are going and in what order of priority.

13. Follow the Platinum Rule

The Golden Rule is good. But in leadership situations, the platinum rule may be even better: "Treat others the way they would like to be treated."

14. Don't Waste People's Time

The best question a leader can ask a subordinate during counseling or performance review is, "How am I wasting your time?" Not everyone will tell you, but cherish the ones that do because they'll help you grow and become successful as a leader.

15. Thank the Invisible People

There are lots of good people doing great work who seldom get thanks because they're invisible. They work so quietly and so competently that they often go unnoticed by the leader.

16. Don't Send "I Don't Trust You" Messages

As I've said before, people who say "I never want to be surprised" or "Check with me before you start anything," or "I'm off on a TDY trip. I'll call in every morning for an update" are sending out very strong "I don't trust you" messages to their subordinates. People who know they aren't trusted will never contribute at their full potential.

17. Serve the Boss, Don't Humor Him/Her

Too many leaders see their biggest job as keeping their bosses happy, getting to the bottom of the inbox, or staying out of trouble. That's not what leadership is about. Leadership is serving the mission, the organization, and your people.

18. Criticize Up, Praise Down

Leaders must occasionally deflect at least some of the bad guidance they get from higher management. Is it being loyal to your boss and to the organization to tell the bosses when they are wearing no clothes? There are ways to be tactful, but honest. Think about it.

19. Be Physically Fit

Everyone has a "health age." If you exercise regularly and watch your diet, you can make yourself four or five years younger than your chronological age. How many of us wouldn't like to be four or five years younger (maybe even twenty years younger)? Would we have done anything differently?

20. Develop Solid Leadership Skills

The best leaders are great at time management and are competent in speed reading, using computers, and the use of brainstorming techniques.

21. Help Your People Understand You

Get your key people together and tell them what your top priorities and your pet peeves are. It's especially important for them to learn very early what really bugs you. They'll appreciate your candor.

22. Concentrate on Performance, Not Just Results

How you get results is important. Ask yourself what it took to gain those great results. Leaders who don't concern themselves about the process and the performance that leads to the results are making a mistake.

23. Maintain a Sense of Outrage

There are many supercool managers who worry too much about keeping their bosses happy. As a result, they never allow themselves to be distressed when the system or the process is doing serious damage to those who work for them. The best leaders get mad occasionally and, using controlled outrage, can often make right the wrongs that are levied upon their people.

24. Beware of Intimidation

Be very careful here. Some bosses allow themselves to be intimidated by outsiders, by their bosses, and even by their subordinates. An intimidated boss can never be a great leader. You have to have an independent mind to make the right choices.

25. Avoid the Activity Trap

Don't confuse being busy with being productive. Without discipline, managers can become slaves to meetings, travel schedules, inboxes, and telephones. They get so wrapped up in the minutiae that they can become "inbox managers" rather than leaders with vision.

26. Beware of the Paul Principle

Too many leaders allow themselves to slowly slide downhill in competence. When they lose touch with the issues, the new technologies, and the people, they fall victim to the Paul principle.

The reality is that politics is part of the job for any leader even when dealing with bosses and employees. Politics is the art of persuasion and influence. A leader who's interested in seeing his vision actually become reality must learn that art. If unable to, they watch their very good ideas fade away, along with the hope for job satisfaction and enhancement.

The future is coming fast. Leaders need to think about it and prepare their people for it. All leaders must work hard to build the future, for that's where they and their people will spend the rest of their lives.

My wife, Anita, and I were discussing work issues and related stresses when the subject of motivation came up. I began to think of situations I'd experienced when review/inspection deadlines (or any other kind for that matter) are pressing and everyone's whining, when you've reminded someone of a task they need to complete for the umpteenth time, or when you've seen the usual suspects delaying the process, and said in frustration, "Why can't they just do their job?"

At the end of the day, it sometimes feels like being a manager or supervisor is like being a glorified babysitter. The duties are the same, but the people are a little larger. You spend your time chasing them around and reminding them of what they're supposed to do and not do.

"The only difference between adults and children is the size of the sandbox." (Evan B. Welch, Dover, NH)

There has to be a better way to manage, right? There is. It's called leadership. I've told you this before, but when you lead, you create an environment where people decide to follow, take responsibility, and are willing to be held accountable. When you manage, you tell people what to do, monitor the progress, and make adjustments as necessary to achieve success. Of course, you should do both, but the more you lead and the less you manage, the more successful you and your employees will be.

Obviously the first step in leadership is determining where you're going. How can people do their jobs if they don't know their purpose? How do their jobs fit into the big picture or even into the next step in the process? People take responsibility much easier when they know what they're responsible for – and that means more than just a list of job tasks.

The second step in leadership is gaining commitment from people to do what they've been hired to do. Make sure you've clearly communicated the job objectives and provided them the necessary tools to do their jobs. If you haven't been clear and specific about what you want them to do, you're going to get mixed results. Make sure they understand why the standards exist and ask them to identify what may keep them from achieving their goals.

The third step in leadership is inviting people to improve the process. Get them involved in finding ways to improve. Don't settle for easy to reach goals. On the other hand, don't kill them with impossibly high goals. If you want to challenge your very best people to stay engaged, stay engaged yourself by looking for and rewarding innovative thinking. Encourage people to look at things with an outside-the-box perspective and ask, "Why do we do it this way?"

The fourth step in leadership is showing you care. The old saying goes, "They don't care how much you know until they know how much you care." If you often find yourself saying, "Why can't they just do their job?" take a look at your own attitude. Have you been empathetic and caring about what is going on with them? We all have one life divided into many segments. It's unrealistic to believe people can leave the rest of their lives outside the main gate (or back entrance). People enjoy working with people they care about. People give to people they care about. People are loyal to people they care about. If people are encouraged to be wholehearted at work, they're more likely to see their work as a piece of their life, not something to avoid.

The fifth step in leadership is helping people find the right fit. Sometimes we put a square peg in a round hole and wonder why it doesn't fit. It's really hard to be successful if you don't have the knowledge, skill, or talent to do a job. Even if you think the job is one that anyone can do, watch for clues that a person might be better suited for a different job. Match talents with learned skills. You'll find that the skill level as well as job satisfaction will be higher.

So the next time you find yourself pulling your hair out asking, "Why can't they just do their job?" stop and ask yourself, "Am I doing everything as a leader to help them do their job successfully?" Remember that just because a job can be done by someone doesn't mean it'll be done by them successfully. You have to lead them by creating an environment where they want to succeed. And sometimes that even means helping them work somewhere else.

I was recently engaged in a debate/discussion over what people value about work (at my age, I think I understand work). Was it the pay, the relationships, or the kinds of work people do that keeps them actively employed? During this conversation, I came to the realization, if I didn't already know it, that everyone has a different core value when describing work. I also found that when people felt that they were owners of the process, they became much more concerned with the success of the organization.

Consequently, I thought about the organization I was involved with and its direction. I asked the question, would you like to get your employees to take more ownership of their jobs and the well-being of your organization? Of course you would, but how to do it is the problem. One answer lies in what they value versus what the organization values.

When we feel stressed, and believe me, there's a lot of that going around. It's often because we're doing things that we don't value highly or we're unable to do the things we do value highly. However, we all make time for things we truly value in life when it becomes a crisis. In the meantime, we tolerate things that don't correspond to what we believe and what we actually do.

It boils down to personal values versus business values. The more similarity you have between your personal values and your business values, the more you'll feel satisfied in your work. Whether you've actually put a label on them or not, people know what's valued at work. The more your values match those values practiced every day, the clearer the values are to the people in the organization. If your organization lives by its values, all business decisions should be within the value structure.

Whether you're a supervisor or an employee, you do yourself and the organization a favor by thinking about what your personal values are and aligning them with your organization. If you're unhappy with where you work and what you do, it could be that you're not able to live your personal values and the incompatibility of that situation is causing you a lot of stress. If you can't resolve that, it might be healthier for you to find another place to work.

If you're in management and you find that your people aren't taking ownership of their jobs, step back and look in the mirror. What are you doing to invite them to take ownership? Are your actions consistent with what the organization says it values? If you say that you value quality, yet you ask people to take shortcuts that make quality inconsistent, people don't believe you value quality. If you say that you value new ideas, but you're too busy to listen to new ideas, people don't think you value ideas, so they stop giving you any. If you say you value innovation, yet you punish mistakes, people believe you value the usual and commonplace.

If you want to build ownership, clearly develop and communicate your corporate values. Then talk to people about their values and try to find harmonious matches. Hire people who have the same values as your organization. Begin a dialogue of how those values translate into how people behave at work. Reinforce positive efforts when values are demonstrated and redirect actions that don't match your values. Soon you'll see a change in direction, and such things as change management and unit compliance inspections will be routine.

Therefore, does living your values increase performance? I think so. I've always tried to apply my values to my work (what little bit I do), and I think that's why I find it hard for me to face retirement. But all good things must end as they say.

Just one more thing!

When asked how I'd cope with not working after nearly fifty-five years on the job, my answer was, "I'm flexible." Although I'm not sure I really am. I'll soon find out. But I got to thinking about it a little more overnight, and I concluded that I need to be more resilient to challenge and change. The world certainly isn't going to come to an end because I'm faced with a new and unfamiliar experience. Not unlike what many organizations are experiencing at this time.

I've discovered through my personal experience that regardless of education, training, previous success, or status, that some people, when confronted with challenging circumstances (like impending inspections/audits, downsizing studies, or poor management), immediately size up the situation and proactively move toward a solution while others become immobilized. The key differentiating factor appears to be something called resilience, the ability to demonstrate both strength and flexibility when faced with dramatically changed expectations. It's not only the capacity to absorb high levels of change but to do it proactively as well.

It's also one of the key characteristics separating successful people from the unsuccessful, yet it's one of the most elusive of human qualities. Oftentimes, you don't know you have it until you need it, such as when dealing with the death of a loved one, going through a divorce, separating from a lifetime of work, preparing for a major audit or some other significantly emotional event.

Can resilience be learned or is it something you're born with? Studies have shown that there are certain behaviors of resilient people that can be learned, for example:

- Have a positive outlook – a sense of security and self-assurance, realization that life is complicated and full of danger but also full of opportunity and teachings.
- Be focused. Have a clear vision of what you want to accomplish in life.
- Be flexible. Be willing to change direction as necessary and as circumstances dictate.
- As a wise philosopher once told me, "The first thing we must do is *get organized.*" Follow a structured approach to deal with and manage ambiguity.
- Be proactive. Make change work for you instead of resisting or fighting it.

I think the three primary characteristics of resilient people are then:

- Acceptance of Reality
  They're able to objectively evaluate the parts of reality that really count for survival and on-going success. They understand their personal strengths and weaknesses and how they can work for or against them in a given set of circumstances.

- A Deep Belief That Life Has Meaning
  They look for patterns, meanings, or keys to learning in adverse circumstances. They have the ability to work through today's situation as a step toward a better tomorrow.

- Ability to Improvise
  They have a sort of inventiveness or creativity that may result in familiar objects being put to unfamiliar uses to make things happen – what most people call thinking outside the box.

How can you learn to be more resilient?

First, realistically assess yourself against those characteristics of resiliency. For weak areas, consciously make an effort to exhibit resilient behaviors the next time you're faced with a significant and unexpected setback.

Second, understand that change is a process with phases that can be worked through. If you're already faced with a challenge, develop and implement a plan to move from where you are today to where you want to be tomorrow. And one way to hold that resilience is to remember that it's the uncertainty of change that causes people the most discomfort, not necessarily the new destination they're trying to reach.

(Definitely my last message!)

INDEX

www.ingramcontent.com/pod-product-compliance
Lightning Source LLC
Chambersburg PA
CBHW031258280526
45784CB00004B/1905